THE
LITURGICAL
MINISTRY ®
SERIES

D1132339

GUIDE FOR
MINISTERS OF LITURGICAL ENVIRONMENT

SECOND EDITION

Corinna Laughlin

Mary Patricia Storms

Paul Turner

LTP

LITURGY
TRAINING
PUBLICATIONS

Nihil Obstat
Rev. Mr. Daniel G. Welter, JD
Chancellor
Archdiocese of Chicago
June 2, 2021

Imprimatur
Most Rev. Robert G. Casey
Vicar General
Archdiocese of Chicago
June 2, 2021

The *Nihil Obstat* and *Imprimatur* are declarations that the material is free from doctrinal or moral error, and thus is granted permission to publish in accordance with c. 827. No legal responsibility is assumed by the grant of this permission. No implication is contained herein that those who have granted the *Nihil Obstat* and *Imprimatur* agree with the content, opinions, or statements expressed.

Cover photo: Matthew Merz © LTP.

Photos on pages 2, 7, 11, 26, 51, 62, and 68: © John Zich; pages 10 and 61: Matthew Merz © LTP; pages 53 and 60: Andrew Lewis © LTP; page 19: Livioandronico / Wikimedia Commons; page 49: L. Simmons © LTP. Line art on pages 32, 34, and 50 by Larry Cope © LTP.

GUIDE FOR MINISTERS OF LITURGICAL ENVIRONMENT, SECOND EDITION © 2021 Archdiocese of Chicago: Liturgy Training Publications, 3949 South Racine Avenue, Chicago IL, 60609; 800-933-1800; fax: 800-933-7094; email: orders@ltp.org; website: www.LTP.org. All rights reserved.

This book is part of the Liturgical Ministry Series®.

This book was edited by Lorie Simmons. Michael A. Dodd was the production editor, Anna Manhart was the designer, and Kari Nichols was the production artist.

25 24 23 22 21   1 2 3 4 5

Printed in the United States of America

Library of Congress Control Number: 2021936115

ISBN: 978-1-61671-592-2

ELMLE2

Contents

Preface

[Christ] is the image of the invisible God.

—Colossians 1:15

To build and adorn a place for worship requires devotion, imagination, and sacrifice. Certainly Jesus understood this. As the Son of God, he surely appreciated the faith that drove volunteers and artisans to decorate the most precious space for worship in his day: the Jerusalem temple. But as he neared the end of his life, Jesus had other things on his mind. He taught that love was the greatest commandment.[1] He raised Lazarus from the dead.[2] He denounced the scribes and Pharisees.[3] He foretold persecutions and terrifying signs that would herald the coming of the Son of Man.[4]

Jerusalem probably dazzled Jesus early in his life, especially as a young boy when he literally lost himself in the temple.[5] But now he was more familiar with the city. He knew its beauty and its deceptions. He knew its hopes and plots. He knew the shortcuts and alleys, the tidy homes and dirty attics. He could have guided first-time visitors through wonders great and small. But Jesus had a date with a cross, and he was in no mood for a holiday.

Others, though, were. Some tourists had arrived, and they were gawking at the temple, while Jesus stood in its shadows. He overheard their comments. One admired the size of the building. Another estimated the cost of the stones. Still another saw how elaborately the interior was decorated. Worshippers had bespangled it with votive offerings, showing their hopes and prayers.[6]

It took money to make places of worship beautiful. People of means saw to it that the temple could boast the finest ornamentation. Their gifts demonstrated the strength of their faith, their love of the arts, and their acceptance of the duty to embellish the holiness of the temple. Their gifts even showed their love for the disadvantaged, whose faith would quicken as they approached this bejeweled place—its signs of respect open to the view of rich and poor alike, challenging all to assign their greatest resources to the praise of God.

These tourists analyzed it all. Jesus could have affirmed their insight. He had done that with the scribe who said loving God and neighbor was more

---

1. Mark 12:29–31.
2. John 11:43–44.
3. Matthew 23:2–3.
4. Luke 21:9–28.
5. Luke 2:46.
6. Luke 21:5.

important than all burnt offerings and sacrifices. Jesus told him, "You are not far from the kingdom of God."[7] That would have been an encouraging word to pass on to these tourists.

Or he could have said, "Yes, and as the incarnate Word, I am especially aware of all the skill and sacrifice that went into making this building and the forging of its decoration."

He even could have said, "You're right. This is the most breathtaking building in the Northern Hemisphere," although they didn't know much about hemispheres in those days.

He could have said something to lift their spirits higher. He could have discoursed on the contribution of art to faith, or on the importance of setting aside a central place where visitors could worship. He could have commanded them to stop looking and start praising the God who so wondrously created the people who so gloriously furbished this temple.

But Jesus didn't say any of that. Instead, having been born in a stark manger, having nowhere to lay his head as an adult, capable of snoozing on a storm-tossed ship at sea, and sensing the weight of his impending crucifixion, an austere Jesus offered a different message:

"All that you see here"—the tourists pause once more to take in the full breadth of the building, not just its individual parts, the stones and votive offerings, but the whole of it, its bearing in the landscape, the reflecting sun, the swelling crowd of worshippers breathing in spirit and breathing out life— "All that you see here," Jesus said, "the days will come when there will not be left a stone upon another stone that will not be thrown down."[8]

It was not the response they were expecting. And it submerged them into a conversation about more important things: when this might happen, how they would know, and how they ought to live.

The temple was a beautiful place to worship. So is a church. When it is properly built and decorously arranged, it moves you. It pulls you out of time and place. It makes you appreciate what God has created. It fills you with the spirit of those who built the edifice. And, most importantly, it makes you ask the questions of eternity: When will Christ come? How will we know? How should I live?

---

7. Mark 12:33–34.
8. Luke 21:6.

How to Use This Resource

Welcome to this guide for ministers of the liturgical environment. Your work lends beauty to the house of God, and it inspires those who gather for worship. This book will support that work.

Much of what you do is temporary. Oh, the building is constructed to last, and the principal furnishings remain steadfast. But flowers bloom and fade. Liturgical colors change with the seasons. The next pastor may have a different idea for the placement of the ambo. Even the more permanent aspects of the edifice are subject to the vagaries of fierce weather, flawed construction, and impulsive vandals. Jesus correctly predicted that not a stone of the temple would be left upon another stone. But the liturgical environment is never about itself. Its fragile nature reaches out to something that endures, and it honors the one who is the same yesterday, today, and tomorrow.

Those tourists whom Jesus met at the temple fixated on the glitz. Even today it is tempting to think of the ministry of liturgical art and architecture as an exercise in show. But very often, less is more. The setting should help draw people into the liturgy: it should accent the places in the environment where important action takes place, and it may echo or highlight the truths and insights that are expressed in the Scripture, prayers, and music of a particular liturgy. The faith and reflection you devote to your ministry will guide both extremes of your work—the simple and the elaborate. Then your work will evoke insights and inspire faith in others.

You work with space and time. Inside a church you decorate the sanctuary differently than the nave. You arrange the reconciliation room more intimately than the narthex.

The seasons affect your work. The liturgical year dictates decoration: the simplicity of Lent contrasts with the exuberance of Christmas. You highlight the image of a saint on a day of local importance. You regulate the landscaping year round.

To do this well, you let the seasons affect *you*. You do this naturally every time you set up a Christmas tree, dress a child for Halloween, or wear the national colors on Independence Day. To adorn the church, you follow the liturgical year by praying over its primary Scriptures and working with its central symbols. You study the readings for the Easter Vigil to choose visual images for the season. You accept a spirit of reflection and remorse in Lent to create a space where others can repent. You remind yourself of the true meaning of Christmas to focus the design of its celebration. You start with the season, you bring it into your heart, and then you express it in the liturgical environment.

On occasion, you have very little time to transform the environment. Advent changes to Christmas overnight. The church is stripped of all excess after Holy Thursday, but it glitters with festivity at the Easter Vigil.

As you go about your work, you put your faith into action. You engage the art of creativity. You imagine visual ways to express an invisible belief, just as artists do. As you do so, people appreciate the ways your faith helps them pray.

This book will help you think about your ministry to the liturgical environment. It will tell you what is important, and why and how this has changed in history. You will find your place in the historical train of illustrious men and women who created and enriched a variety of places for prayer. You will receive some practical advice. You will learn about the various ways to transform liturgical space according to the seasons, the rites, and the people of different cultures who celebrate them. As you make the church more appealing to the human eye, you can make it more conducive to the divine mysteries.

You will also receive some spiritual guidance. This book will help you pray about your work, reflect on the Scriptures and prayers of the Mass, discern the primary symbols, and connect contemporary needs to the tradition of the Church. It will support your spirit of service and your life as a disciple of Christ.

> In order to communicate the message entrusted to us by Christ, the church needs art. Art must make perceptible, and as far as possible attractive, the world of the spirit, of the invisible, of God. It must therefore translate into meaningful terms that which is in itself ineffable. Art has a unique capacity to take one or another facet of the message and translate it into colors, shapes, and sounds that nourish the intuition of those who look or listen. It does so without emptying the message itself of its transcendent value and its aura of mystery.
>
> —Pope John Paul II,
> *Letter to Artists*, 12

When King David told God he wanted to build a temple, God practically laughed at him. God had never lived in a house before.[1] God does not need a building, but *we* need buildings. We need sacred spaces that blend nature's substances with human ingenuity, spaces that call us back to the center of who and why we are. When you prepare the sacred space of your church for worship, you are also helping to prepare the hearts of the worshipers. You are helping believers to feel at home with God and in awe of God.

---

1. 2 Samuel 7:6.

About the Authors

Corinna Laughlin wrote chapter 1. She is the pastoral assistant for liturgy at St. James Cathedral in Seattle, Washington, and liturgy consultant for the Archdiocese of Seattle. She has written extensively on the liturgy for Liturgy Training Publications and has contributed articles to *Pastoral Liturgy*®, *Ministry and Liturgy,* and other publications. She holds a doctorate in English from the University of Washington.

Mary Patricia Storms wrote the description and explanation of the duties of ministers of liturgical environment in chapter 3 and most of "Frequently Asked Questions." She also provided the resources list and glossary. She is a pastoral associate for adult formation at Our Lady of the Presentation Parish in Lee's Summit, Missouri. There, in addition to directing a variety of adult faith formation programs, she continues to practice and develop her expertise in liturgical environment. A graduate of Rockhurst University and the University of Missouri–Kansas City, she holds an MA in curriculum and instruction.

Paul Turner wrote the preface, "How to Use This Resource," and chapters 2 and 4. He is the pastor of the Cathedral of the Immaculate Conception in Kansas City, Missouri, and the director of the Office of Divine Worship for the Diocese of Kansas City–St. Joseph. He holds a doctorate in sacred theology from Sant'Anselmo in Rome and is the author of many pastoral and theological resources. He serves as a facilitator for the International Commission on English in the Liturgy.

Questions for Reflection and Discussion

1. Why have you agreed to serve as a minister of the liturgical environment at your church? What gifts, skills, or interests have brought you to this ministry?

2. What do you hope to gain in your understanding of the theology and function of the ministry through this book?

Chapter 1

Your Ministry and the Liturgy

The liturgy is the source and summit of the Christian life.

—*Lumen gentium*, 11

You're reading this book because you have felt a call to serve your parish as a minister of the liturgical environment. Or, perhaps you already serve in this way and want to take a fresh look at the principles and best practices of the ministry. One thing is certain: you're reading this book because liturgy matters to you.

What Is Liturgy?

Dictionaries will tell you, in one way or another, that *liturgy* is a collection of rites used in public worship. And that is true. But there is much more to liturgy than that. The word *liturgy* comes from a Greek word meaning "public work" or "work of the people." That hits nearer the mark: liturgy is a special kind of work in which the divine and human come together; we do something, and, more importantly, God does something. Liturgy is not a thing; liturgy is an *event*. So let's ask a different question: What does liturgy *do*?

Liturgy gathers us in the presence of God. In speaking of the Eucharist, the second-century *Didache* emphasizes gathering: "Even as this broken bread was scattered over the hills, and was gathered together and became one, so let Your Church be gathered together from the ends of the earth into Your kingdom."[1] Here the Eucharistic bread, formed from many grains of wheat, is an image of what we are to be: disparate individuals who become something new— a worshiping assembly. In the Bible, the gathering of God's people is a sign of the in-breaking of the kingdom of God. Think of Isaiah's vision of a great

In the liturgy, by means of signs perceptible to the senses, human sanctification is signified and brought about in ways proper to each of these signs.

—*Sacrosanctum concilium*, 7

banquet on a mountaintop.[2] Think of Jesus feeding the multitudes[3] or of the disciples gathered in prayer in the upper room on the first Pentecost.[4] When God gathers his people together, something happens. The same is true of the liturgy. Before a word has been spoken or a note sung, the liturgy is already a sign of the kingdom of God because it gathers us together.

---

1. *The Didache: The Lord's Teaching Through the Twelve Apostles to the Nations*, 9. https://www.newadvent.org/fathers/0714.htm; accessed March 25, 2021.
2. See Isaiah 25:6–9.
3. See Matthew 14:13–21, Mark 6:30–44, Luke 9:10–17, and John 6:1–15.
4. See Acts of the Apostles 2:1–11.

Liturgy helps form us into a community. The act of being together at table, of sharing the Word of God, of being one voice in our sung and spoken prayers, has an impact on us. It is through this shared action in the liturgy that we learn to recognize ourselves as a family of believers, the Body of Christ, and to be united in our action outside of the church as well. We join in the liturgy because we are a community, but the reverse is also true: without the liturgy, we are not a community at all.

Liturgy is both common and cosmic. The liturgy takes the most ordinary things—our bodies and voices, light and darkness, water and fire, bread, wine, and oil, time itself—and, through the action of the Holy Spirit, transforms all of these into God's very presence. The liturgy teaches us to see that the entire universe is marked with the presence of Christ. The "seeds" of God are everywhere in the world. The stuff of our holiness is not far away, remote, or arcane. The common is holy.

Christian liturgy is always about the paschal mystery. At the heart of all Christian prayer is the paschal mystery— that is, the life, death, and resurrection of Christ. Whether our prayer is the Mass, the Liturgy of the Hours, a saint's day, a sacrament—whether it is Advent or Christmas Time, Lent, Triduum, or Easter Time—the liturgy is always about the paschal mystery. Why is the paschal mystery so important? Because, in the words of St. Paul, "if Christ has not been raised, your faith is vain; you are still in your sins."[5] The paschal mystery is the fulcrum of history and the dynamic reality which gives meaning to our lives and enlivens our worship. We gather for liturgy in order to be plunged, again and again, into the paschal mystery.

In the liturgy, we meet Christ. We know that Christ is always close to those who believe: Jesus said, "whoever loves me will keep my word, and my Father will love him, and we will come to him and make our dwelling with him."[6] But, in the celebration of the Eucharist, Christ is present to us in a special way. In fact, the Church highlights *four* presences of Christ at Mass. Christ is present in the community gathered for prayer; Christ comes to us in each other. Christ is present in the priest, who acts *in persona Christi*, in the person of Christ, in the Mass. Christ is present in the word proclaimed: "When the

---

5. I Corinthians 15:17.
6. John 14:23.

Sacred Scriptures are read in the Church, God himself speaks to his people, and Christ, present in his word, proclaims the Gospel."[7] And in a unique way, Christ is present in the consecrated bread and wine, his true Body and Blood, shared with us in the Eucharist. Through our participation in this mystery, we meet Christ in many ways and we become what we receive: the Body of Christ.[8]

Liturgy is the worship of the Church. The liturgy is not free-form. As the official prayer of the Universal Church, it is governed by universal norms. Most of the texts we hear at Mass—with some significant exceptions, like the homily and the universal prayer—are written down and are the same the world over. Not only the words of liturgy, but most of the actions are the same everywhere: standing, sitting, and kneeling. The liturgical books include many rubrics (from the Latin word for "red," because these instructions are sometimes printed in red ink), which give instructions for how and where each part of the liturgy happens. All of this should remind us that the liturgy does not belong to any one person, priest, or parish. The liturgy is the Church's prayer. But, that does not mean that it is not *our* prayer too. In the words of the Second Vatican Council, the liturgy is "the outstanding means whereby the faithful may express in their lives and manifest to others the mystery of Christ and the real nature of the true Church."[9] Liturgy is our means of expression with Christ and about Christ. In other words, liturgy is the language we speak as Catholics.

The liturgy is richly varied. While the liturgy is carefully governed by liturgical books, it is never monotone. It is constantly changing, with different readings for every day of the year, and different prayers for most days. Through the liturgical year, the Church invites us to meditate on different aspects of the mystery of Christ, from his conception to his second coming. The liturgy is colorful!

The preeminent manifestation of the Church is present in the full, active participation of all God's holy people in these liturgical celebrations, especially in the same eucharist.

—*Sacrosanctum concilium*, 41

The Eucharist is the most important of the Church's liturgies, but it is not our only liturgy. The liturgies of the Church also include rites like those in the *Rite of Christian Initiation of Adults* and the *Order of Christian Funerals*. They include celebrations of the other sacraments, from baptism, confirmation, and Eucharist to anointing and penance, matrimony, and holy orders. In addition, the Liturgy of the Hours, prayed daily by deacons, priests, bishops, religious, and many laypeople, is part of the Church's liturgy, sanctifying the hours of each day with prayer to God.

---

7. *General Instruction of the Roman Missal* (GIRM), 29.
8. See *Sacrosanctum concilium* (SC), 7.
9. SC, 2.

Liturgy is different from devotion. The Church has a rich and wonderful array of devotional prayer—novenas, chaplets, the Rosary, the Way of the Cross, among others—which can enrich our prayer and bring us closer to Christ and to his Mother. The Rosary has a special place in the life of the Church, for, in the words of St. John Paul II, it "serves as an excellent introduction and a faithful echo of the Liturgy, enabling people to participate fully and interiorly in it and to reap its fruits in their daily lives."[10] These devotions can enrich, but must never replace, our participation in the liturgy.

Liturgy both reflects and shapes our faith. A medieval scholar expressed this in a phrase that has become famous: *lex orandi, lex credendi*, which can loosely be translated as "the law of prayer shapes the law of belief." In other words, the way we pray informs our theology. If you look at the footnotes in the documents of the Second Vatican Council, and in the *Catechism of the Catholic Church*, you'll notice that the sources cited for key teachings not only include the Bible and teachings of popes and councils, but prayers from the Mass. Liturgy is a school of prayer and a school of faith, teaching us to believe with the Church.

The medieval adage is often extended to read *lex orandi, lex credendi, lex vivendi*—"law of life." The way we pray shapes what we believe—and the way we live our lives. Authentic worship and faith lead to discipleship. If it doesn't, it means the transforming power of the liturgy is not really reaching us. As Pope Benedict XVI has written, "A Eucharist which does not pass over into the concrete practice of love is intrinsically fragmented."[11]

Liturgy really matters. *Sacrosanctum concilium* of the Second Vatican Council had this to say about liturgy: "The liturgy is the summit toward which the activity of the Church is directed; at the same time it is the font from which all the Church's power flows."[12] Liturgy is both source and summit, culmination and starting-place. All the preaching and evangelizing the Church does is meant to draw people to Christ in the celebration of the Eucharist. At the same time, though, the Eucharist is not a stopping place. Liturgy is the fountain from which we draw strength to do Christ's work in the world. Liturgy gathers us; liturgy also sends us forth. And if liturgy fails to do that, there is a problem. "We cannot delude ourselves," wrote St. John Paul II, "by our mutual love and, in particular, by our concern for those in need we will be recognized as true followers of Christ. . . . This will be the criterion by which the authenticity of our Eucharistic celebrations is judged."[13]

---

10. *Rosarium Virginis Mariae*, 4.
11. *Deus caritas est*, 14.
12. SC, 10.
13. *Mane nobiscum Domine*, 28.

The Privilege to Serve

Liturgical ministers have the wonderful privilege of helping others participate in this transforming reality we call the Church's liturgy. Whether we are proclaiming a Scripture reading, taking up the collection, distributing Communion, carrying a candle, or preparing the liturgical environment, our goal is the same: to help others find in the liturgy what we have found—a community of believers, a school of holiness, a place of encounter with Jesus Christ. When we go to Mass, we never come out the same, because liturgy is meant to change us. No wonder, then, that the Church puts such emphasis on participation in the liturgy. If we participate fully, consciously, and actively in the liturgy, we cannot fail to be transformed, and do our part to transform the world we live in. As liturgical ministers, we are called to do just that, and to help others do the same.

Questions for Reflection and Discussion

1. How is praying with a community different than praying on your own? Why do you think Jesus calls us to pray in both ways?

2. What liturgies of the Church do you participate in on a regular basis?

3. Where and when do you feel closest to Christ?

4. Think about the ways Christ is present in the liturgy and in the world. Think of a time when you have felt Christ's presence in these places.

5. How does participating in the liturgy affect your life outside of the liturgy?

Chapter 2

The Meaning and History
of Your Ministry

[The church building] must be expressive of the presence
of God and suited for the celebration of the sacrifice of Christ,
as well as reflective of the community that celebrates there.

—*Built of Living Stones*, 16

A Minister of Sacramental Beauty

You have felt a call to care for sacred spaces and to adorn them so that the mysteries we celebrate are more inviting and understandable to the people of God. You are not simply a decorator, flower arranger, needleworker, handy person, or tidier. You may play all of those roles in the course of your work, but you will do so with insight into the way the liturgy helps us encounter Christ through the things of the earth. You will do so as a minister. Seeing the presence of God in the material—understanding the sacramentality and spiritual beauty of physical things—that will be your specialty as you use those things to draw the assembly into the liturgy and recognize Christ's presence.

Your training will give you confidence and make you effective in your work, but the real grounding for your participation in this ministry comes from your baptism. After you were washed in the baptismal water, the priest anointed you with chrism and proclaimed that you were now joined to the Body of Christ as priest, prophet, and king. Your baptism empowers you to share in Christ's gifts and to do his work in the world. It is your baptismal priesthood that qualifies you in this ministry of the Church. As one who will devote yourself to fashioning the sacramental beauty of the liturgical environment, you will want to know more about the meaning and history of the sacred spaces you arrange.

The Church Building: Setting for Sunday Mass

The main reason we build churches is for the Sunday Eucharist. We use them for many other events—from festive weddings to private prayer. But the primary design and decoration of a church depends on what we need for Sunday Mass.

The building gets its name from the people who gather there: church. We are living stones built into a spiritual house.[1] We are the temple of God,

---

1. 1 Peter 2:5.

and that temple is holy.[2] We gather as the Body of Christ, and he is our priest.[3] We are church. So is our building.

The building gives the community a space where it meets God. In the Catholic tradition, we do not perform weddings in parks or baptisms in lakes. We gather at our churches because they represent the people of faith, and they are our principal centers for encountering God together. Other spaces are sacred. Roadside markers designate the places where accident victims lost their lives. The home of one's youth is replete with memory. A view of the ocean convinces the observer of nature's might. But churches are special. They are built and consecrated for the purpose of meeting God. Generations of worshippers have prayed for a multitude of reasons, and their faith continues to sanctify the hallowed space of a church.

Catholics design churches according to the needs of the Sunday Eucharist. The altar occupies a central area. The ambo stands where people can see and hear the one who reads the Word of God. There is space for receiving Communion. The entire building provides suitable seating for all who come to pray. The arrangement facilitates public processions and quiet devotion. It is fixed, yet flexible.

The building complements the symbols of our worship: bread and wine, which we offer in sacrifice and consume in a sacred meal; water, which promises life and cleansing; oil, which helps us pray for healing, protection, and grace; fire, which reminds us of the risen Christ, who shatters the darkness of sin; the cross, which humbles us even as it announces redemption; incense,

---

2. 1 Corinthians 3:16.
3. "The liturgy is considered as an exercise of the priestly office of Jesus Christ . . . the whole public worship is performed by the Mystical Body of Jesus Christ, that is, by the Head and his members" SC, 7.

which bears our prayers aloft and fills the building with the sweet aroma of holiness; and the assembly of God's people, who call this church their home.

The entire complex serves the primary spiritual needs of the Catholic community. It does this especially well when care is given to its components.

The Nave

The people who come for worship take their places in the area called the nave.[4] The word is related to the English words "navy" and "nautical" because early examples bore some semblance to the hold of a ship.

The celebration of the Eucharist assumes the presence of people in the nave. In the Order of Mass, the part of the missal that describes how a typical Mass flows, the first two words are *"Populo congregato."*[5] They mean "Once the people have gathered." Nothing else happens at Mass until the congregation is there. The place where they assemble is the nave.

The Sanctuary

The primary actions of the Mass take place in the sanctuary, a spacious area separated from the nave by its elevation or ornamentation.[6] People in the nave should be able to see and hear what happens in the sanctuary.

The sanctuary holds the primary furnishings needed for the celebration of the Eucharist: the altar, the ambo, and the chair.

The Altar

The altar resembles a table because it is the place where the sacrifice of the cross is made present and from which the gathered assembly shares the sacred banquet of the Body and Blood of Christ.[7] It should be the center of attention.

The Ambo

The Word of God is proclaimed from the ambo, which resembles a lectern or pulpit.[8] It should be large enough to accommodate the *Lectionary for Mass* and the *Book of the Gospels*. Usually, it is equipped with a microphone to assist the audible proclamation of the Scriptures, the preaching, and the universal prayer or prayer of the faithful.

---

4. *Built of Living Stones* (BLS), 51–53.
5. *Order of Mass*, 1.
6. GIRM, 295; BLS, 54–55.
7. GIRM, 296; BLS, 56–59.
8. GIRM, 309; BLS, 61–62.

The Chair

The priest who celebrates the Mass has his own place to sit.[9] That may not seem noteworthy, but the presider's chair signifies the role of the priest in the community, and it is the place where certain actions of the Mass occur.

The priest is shepherd and servant of the people. His chair has the same function as the head of the dining room table or of a company's board room. We even call the person who leads a committee a "chair."

The presider's chair is also the place where the priest first addresses the people, where he offers some of the prayers at the Mass, and even where he may preach. The chair means something even when the priest is not sitting there. He stands in front of the chair to pray the collect, the prayer that concludes the Introductory Rites of the Mass. His nearness to the chair shows he is the leader, and his posture shows his respect for God.

Other Seating

If there is a deacon, he has a chair near the priest. If there are altar servers or other ministers, they have seats in the sanctuary, but these should be less prominent than those for the priest and deacon.

The choir usually leads the singing from a special area.[10] Sometimes only one song leader or cantor takes on this responsibility. Singers and musicians are part of the assembly of the faithful and their location best makes that clear. A good location facilitates their role as leaders of the assembly's song. The one who leads the responsorial psalm may do so from the ambo, but other music is led from a lectern, music stand, or other adjunct place.

Communion Stations

The priest and other ministers of Communion leave the sanctuary to distribute Communion at stations where the people arrive in procession.[11] Usually, the Communion stations are in the parts of the nave nearest the altar; for example, at the head of the aisles. The primary liturgical documents never describe them in any detail, but Communion stations need to be spacious enough to accommodate the steady movement of the people, yet intimate enough to enhance the sacramental encounter of each communicant with the Body and Blood of Christ.

Cross and Candles

A cross depicting the crucified body of Jesus should be on or close to the altar, or be carried in the entrance procession and stationed there.[12] The physical relationship between the altar and the cross allows the image of the crucified

---

9. GIRM, 310; BLS, 63–65.
10. BLS, 88–90.
11. GIRM, 160.
12. GIRM, 117, 122, 308; BLS, 91.

Christ to interpret the meaning of the actions on the altar. During some Masses, a minister will incense both the altar and the cross. This action assumes they stand in proximity to each other. Still, it should be clear that the altar is more central to the liturgy than the cross.[13]

Candles sit on or near the altar before Mass begins, or they are carried there in the entrance procession.[14] Originally, candles served a practical function: they illumined an otherwise dark area of the building. But now they are signs of reverence and festivity.[15]

Vestments and Vessels

The priest, deacon, and servers vest for the Mass. Clergy wear colors that announce the occasion, feast, or season being celebrated. Vestments are most effective when they are clean, beautiful, and functional. Ministers need vestments that fit. They should form a coherent part of the visual tapestry in the sanctuary. They should draw attention to the action of the Mass, not to the ministers.

Various vessels and cloths are needed. These, too, should be functional and beautiful.[16]

Various colors of cloth are needed to match the colors of the liturgical seasons.

Other Tables

A credence table holds many of the items needed for the Mass, such as extra cups for communion, a ewer of water, and various small cloths. The credence table usually sits near a sanctuary wall. It does not belong adjacent to the altar, where it may detract from the significance of the central table.

Another small table usually stands near the back of the nave. On it are placed the bread and wine for Mass. A procession of these gifts will usually start from this table and end at the entrance to the sanctuary. The primary liturgical documents never mention this table, but nearly every church uses one.

The Tabernacle

The consecrated eucharistic bread that remains after Mass is kept under lock and key in a sturdy chest called a tabernacle. It usually resembles an ornate box, although it has had other forms. The communion breads are kept in reserve so that designated ministers may carry them to those who are too sick to worship at church. Catholics believe that the real presence of Christ endures

---

13. GIRM, 296.
14. GIRM, 117, 122.
15. GIRM, 307; BLS, 92–93.
16. GIRM, 327–347; BLS, 164–165.

in the consecrated bread. For this reason the tabernacle is a paramount place for devotional practice in the church. A worshipper genuflects when approaching or passing the tabernacle outside of Mass.

The tabernacle should be situated in a prominent place either in a chapel suitable for private prayer or in the sanctuary. It should not be placed on the altar on which the Mass is celebrated.[17] Broadly speaking, it is possible to celebrate Mass without a tabernacle. The bread and wine brought to the altar may be consecrated there and entirely consumed by the worshippers. The nobility of the tabernacle and the centrality of the altar should be clear to all who participate in the Mass.

The Font

Baptism in the Catholic Church may be administered by immersion or pouring, though it "is performed in the most expressive way by triple immersion in the baptismal water."[18] The place for baptism is called the font, and it should be suitable for exercising both options.[19]

Baptisms may take place during Mass, and they have a pivotal role at the Easter Vigil, when they help express the implications of the resurrection of Christ. Even when baptisms take place apart from Mass, they may be witnessed by a large group of family and friends. For these reasons, the font belongs where people can see it and hear the words of the rite. Some older churches have small baptistries inside the front door. Today these are usually less suitable for the methods of baptizing and the crowd of witnesses.

For adult immersions, a font needs to be large enough to accommodate at least one adult if not also the baptizing minister and the godparent. The immersion of a child can be done in the same font or in a large bowl of water.

---

17. GIRM, 314, 315; BLS, 70–73.
18. *Catechism of the Catholic Church* (CCC), 1239.
19. BLS, 66–69.

Fonts have taken a variety of shapes. Some are round, suggesting a womb for rebirth. Some are rectangular, like the tomb from which one rises again. Others are cruciform, for Christians are baptized into the death and Resurrection of Christ. Still others are octagonal. Sunday is considered not just the first but the eighth day of the week. The number eight suggests a time outside of time, the eternal life in which baptism participates.

The Ambry

The sacred oils used in the sacraments are reserved in a special area in the church; often these sit on shelves in a box called an ambry. Whenever a priest anoints the sick, he uses the oil of the sick. Whenever a priest or deacon anoints a child or an adult prior to baptism, he uses the oil of catechumens. Chrism, the perfumed oil, is used for postbaptismal anointing, confirmation, the ordination of a priest and a bishop, and for the anointing of a new altar and the walls of a new church.

In older churches, a place for the oils was often embedded in a wall of the sacristy, out of view from the assembly. Today some churches place the oils in a glass-paneled ambry where they can be seen by the faithful. Moreover, today the ambry is often located near the font because two of the oils are used in the rites of initiation.

The Narthex

Inside the main exterior doors some churches have a large gathering area, sometimes called the narthex.[20] Arriving worshippers may meet and greet one another there. They begin the weekly process of forming themselves as one body of believers who will worship, sing, make responses, listen, and observe silences together. After the service, many will linger to catch up with one another and make plans for the week ahead.

The narthex is also a place where a parish may make various resources available. Bulletins, information flyers, boxes to collect food and clothing for the needy, tables for promoting parochial activities, and even coffee and donuts can be offered in this common area. The narthex is a place for sharing information and building community. It is the gateway into worship and the springboard into service.

The Sacristy

Items for the liturgy are stored in a room called the sacristy. Often there are two of these. One is for the vesting of the ministers. The other is for the storage and cleaning of vessels. The vesting sacristy may be located near the door of the church, so that the newly robed ministers have ready access to the start

---

20. BLS, 95–97.

of the procession. The working sacristy may be located closer to the sanctuary, to facilitate the disposition of the vessels.

The working sacristy usually has running water for cleansing. It is also equipped with a sacrarium, a special sink with a pipe that goes into the earth. After the vessels have been purified by a priest or deacon, water from the first washing is usually poured down the sacrarium.

The Reconciliation Room

Penitents seeking absolution usually confess to a priest in a private area in the church.[21] They have a choice of naming their sins to him face to face or anonymously. Traditional confessionals provided sufficient space for a seated priest and a kneeling penitent. Many churches now house reconciliation rooms where the priest and penitent may both sit and face each other.

Such rooms have the feel of a small chapel or counseling area. They more generously allow the priest to greet the penitent warmly and with kindness as the Rite of Penance suggests.[22]

Reconciliation rooms and confessionals may be in the nave, but they may also be set apart from it. Confessions may be heard during Mass, but it will be less distracting to Mass-goers and penitents alike if they take place in separate areas or at separate times.

Devotional Areas

A number of other areas support the devotion of the people. These spaces are traditionally found in Catholic churches, but they have a more tangential relationship to our primary purpose for gathering: the celebration of the Mass.

Holy Water Stoups

Holy water stoups are placed near the door of the church. Upon entering the building, the faithful usually dip some fingers in the water and make the sign of the cross. The ritual reminds them of their baptism and serves as a purification rite.[23]

Most people sign themselves with water again as they leave the building. This practice never appears in the official liturgical books, but most Catholics do it instinctively as a way of keeping with them some of the holiness of the space, and perhaps to strengthen their resolve to live out their baptism as they reenter the secular space of the world.

---

21. BLS, 103–105.
22. *Rite of Penance*, 41.
23. *Ceremonial of Bishops*, 110.

Statues and Pictures of Christ and the Saints

Statues and pictures of Christ and the saints may adorn the walls or fill niches in the nave or other areas. By gazing on the images of the saints, Catholics connect with heroes and intercessors who inspire and assist their spiritual journey. It is especially common to find images of the Sacred Heart of Jesus and the Blessed Virgin Mary. These visible images remind us of the invisible communion of saints with whom we gather at every Mass.

Some churches have moved images of the saints to the periphery, lest the private nature of these devotions compete with the common nature of the liturgy.

Votive Candles

Votive candles are usually situated in areas adjacent to images of the saints. Many Catholics observe the pious tradition of saying a prayer before an image, making a donation, and then lighting a candle before they leave. The candle represents an offering of beauty to lengthen the donors' presence and to bolster their prayer.

Stations of the Cross

Stations of the Cross are usually found on the walls of the nave. Most churches schedule common celebrations of the stations on Fridays of Lent, but these images adorn our sacred spaces year round, providing a narrative context for the cross of Christ.

Other Spaces

The exterior of a church, especially its facade, often carries religious images or inscriptions.

Windows, especially those of stained glass, are traditional areas for decoration. During the Middle Ages, when illiteracy prevented many believers from reading the Bible on their own, stained-glass windows taught them the foundations of their faith. They functioned as storyboards for the lives of the saints and canvases for geometric configurations. Above all, they colored the light, and they inspired a sense of devotion through the imaginative use of beauty.

Some churches have a lawn, square, or plaza in front. In pleasant weather, these serve the same function as a narthex: they allow people to greet one another before and after a service. In some areas, the land around a church doubles as a kind of public park, a churchyard through which people pass during the week. Some churches serve the community by tending gardens in these places or by providing a venue for casual or planned communication.

The church exterior presents more opportunities for seasonal decoration. It alerts people to the time of year or a festival day even before they enter the building.

The atmosphere inside a church may also help establish an environment. The draping of cloths, the shining of lights, and the wafting of incense may all conspire to celebrate a special occasion. Even the absence of these embellishments may create a useful austerity that defines certain occasions for worship.

The areas of a building and objects for the liturgy are used year round. But there are some specific occasions that need the special attention of ministers of the liturgical environment.

The Church Building as a Setting for Other Liturgical Occasions

The Liturgy of the Hours

Some religious communities gather to pray several times a day. The Liturgy of the Hours regularly takes place in monasteries and convents, but any parish church is encouraged to offer at least Morning Prayer and Evening Prayer. One traditional seating arrangement divides the assembly into two halves facing each other (called an antiphonal arrangement); the sides alternate singing the verses of the psalms so that everyone may both pray and listen to God's Word. Adaptations in physical arrangement, however, may be made.[24]

Rites of Christian Initiation of Adults (the Catechumenate)

The expansive series of rites that make up the Christian initiation of adults have special requirements. During the Rite of Acceptance into the order of catechumens, unbaptized adults and children of catechetical age become formally designated as catechumens in preparation for baptism. The liturgy is to begin outside the nave in an area large enough to accommodate a group of the faithful, and where all can participate in dialogue with the priest or deacon who presides.[25]

During many prebaptismal rites, a minister prays over catechumens. They need a space to congregate. Some parishes have them enter the sanctuary; others use the aisles or the communion station areas. Catechumens and their sponsors need appropriate spaces to stand as one and to be seen by those praying for them.

Communal Penance or Reconciliation Services

At times—usually during Advent and Lent—a parish community will gather for the communal celebration of reconciliation with individual confession and

---

24. BLS, 115.
25. *Rite of Christian Initiation of Adults* (RCIA), 48.

absolution. Several confessors usually assist. During the service, people approach one of them. They all need private spaces for this encounter. Stations may be established in the sanctuary, at the head of the aisles, or around the periphery, as long as conversations there will not be overheard.

Communal Anointing of the Sick

The sick of the parish may be anointed in groups, even during Sunday Mass.[26] They may need special seating, perhaps in pews near the front, where they have adequate support, and where the priest may approach them to impose hands and anoint their forehead and palms. On all days the church should be accessible to those in wheelchairs and others with special needs.

Marriage

Engaged couples will probably want to decorate the church for their wedding.[27] Sometimes they add elaborate decorations for a one-hour ceremony, and then the church is restored to its normal seasonal decor for other services that day.

During the ceremony, the bride and groom need proper seating. They may take places with the assembly or even in the sanctuary.[28]

Wakes and Funerals

When a member of the community dies, people gather at church to pay their respects. Although many funeral homes offer rooms for a wake service, the Vigil for the Deceased may properly take place in the parish church. There should be adequate room for the viewing of a body. A church is naturally prepared with the other requirements for this liturgical service: an ambo, a chair, seating for the mourners, and participation aids.[29]

During the liturgical year the Church unfolds the whole mystery of Christ, from his incarnation and birth through his passion, death, and resurrection to his ascension, the day of Pentecost, and the expectation of his coming in glory. In its celebration of these mysteries, the Church makes these sacred events present to the people of every age.

—*Built of Living Stones*, 122 (see *Sacrosanctum concilium*, 102)

At the funeral, the mourners need space to receive the body and cover the coffin with a pall. The aisle should be wide enough for pall bearers to escort the coffin toward the altar, with sufficient space there for a minister to walk around it with incense.

Eucharistic Exposition and Adoration

The ceremony commonly called "benediction" summons believers to adore the real presence of Christ in the Blessed Sacrament during periods of silence,

---

26. BLS, 109.
27. BLS, 106–108.
28. BLS, 108.
29. BLS, 110–114.

song, prayer, and readings from Scripture.[30] Candelabra are traditionally set in the sanctuary. A monstrance that displays the consecrated host is prepared for the altar.

The Church Building throughout the Liturgical Year

The liturgical calendar sets the direction for many changeable aspects of the environment.[31] During Advent, many parishes set up a wreath, which is blessed on the first Sunday of the season. At Christmas the faithful may want to pray quietly before a crèche. If the optional memorial of St. Blaise is celebrated on February 3, candles will be prepared for the annual blessing of throats. As Lent begins, ashes from old palm branches are placed in containers and set on a table near the presider's chair. On Palm Sunday, branches will be supplied to the assembly.

During the Paschal Triduum, several needs arise.[32] For the washing of the feet on Holy Thursday, the priest will need a pitcher of water, a bowl, and a towel. At the end of that liturgy, consecrated breads will be placed in a special area of reservation suitably decorated. That area may be outside the nave.

On Good Friday, the clergy may begin the liturgy by lying prostrate in the sanctuary. They should have room to stretch out. A cross is prepared for the adoration of the faithful.

For the Easter Vigil, a fire large enough to dispel the darkness of night should be set ablaze, preferably outdoors. A paschal candle needs to be prepared. There should be adequate space for the baptisms; a temporary font may be set up in the sanctuary if the church does not have a suitable font.

A Manifold Beauty

Beauty should govern the environment of a church. God is the source of all that is good, and things that are beautiful lead worshippers back to God. No religious work of art should draw more attention to the artist than to God, the source of creation. They all serve a purpose: enhancing religious worship.

No one style of art from any culture, region, or period of time can possibly express all that Christians believe.[33] For this reason, the Church has

> Liturgical art and architecture reflect and announce the presence of the God who calls the community to worship and invite believers to raise their minds and hearts to the One who is the source of all beauty and truth.
>
> —*Built of Living Stones*, 44

wisely encouraged the construction of buildings in multiple styles, the incorporation of a variety of artistic techniques, and the authentic use of materials indigenous to the regions of the world where Christianity has flowered. This

---

30. See the *Order for the Solemn Exposition of the Holy Eucharist*.
31. BLS, 122–129.
32. BLS, 81.
33. BLS, 38–45.

multiplicity of form refracts the eternal simplicity and complexity of God. It shows the manifold influence of the Holy Spirit.

Art and architecture continue to evolve with the culture. They rely on new insights, new technologies, and practical accommodations to available space. Although many Catholics continue to benefit from the longstanding art forms and styles of the past, today's artists need encouragement to contribute their gifts and so help their contemporaries worship in ways that meet modern needs.

History

Throughout history, the Catholic Church has demonstrated constant support for the development of art and architecture. Some religious art is highly liturgical, such as the design and furnishing of churches. Other art is more devotional, such as the making of objects for personal prayer. In all cases, Christianity has found the Church to be a welcome companion in the history of the visual arts. A few highlights will illustrate the patterns and shifts that explain the coexistence of various styles today.

The first Christians gathered for worship in intimate settings. Participants were few, buildings were small, and the needs for the Eucharist were simple. In those early days, Christians worshipped in large homes—in a dining room or an enclosed courtyard. Pools of water provided a spot for baptisms. In these settings the Eucharist resembled a family meal—people ate reclining or sitting up, enjoying one another's company at common prayer.

Leaders in the Roman Empire were adherents of the state religion or other ancient cults, and they persecuted Christians, but in 313 Emperor Constantine ruled that the new religion would be tolerated, and then even promoted. The number of worshippers increased, and special buildings had to be constructed for them.

One model for large public buildings at the time was the basilica. People gathered in these rectangular enclosed halls to hear speeches, transact business, and appeal for judgment in the courts. One end of the building closed with an apse, a semicircular space roofed by a half dome. This area was a focal point for activity and provided acoustical assistance to the human voice. Pillars held the roof up high over the long central vessel of the building (the nave) and formed the border of its lower-roofed side aisles. Windows pierced the upper registers of the high walls above the pillars, flooding the nave with light.

When Christians needed large buildings for worship, they adopted the basilica form. They oriented the buildings toward the east, the home of the rising sun and a symbol of the resurrection. They placed a chair for the presider in the apse, so that his voice could be heard more easily. Readings were proclaimed from an elevated place for the same reason. A freestanding table in the apse served as the altar.

Built in the fifth century, the Church of St. Sabina is one of the early basilica-style churches in Rome.

The intimacy of the house church could not be recreated in the larger space, but the presence of more worshippers strengthened the solemnity of the entire ceremony. Processions naturally evolved. Singing became more central. Roles within the liturgy crystallized and diversified.

Baptistries also underwent an organic development. What began as a pool of water in the courtyard of a house church became a building separate from the basilica. As the church went indoors, so did the font. Baptistries were large enough to immerse or partially submerge an adult in the presence of ministers and a number of witnesses. In a time and place where people bathed in public, new Christians were probably baptized in the nude. This may have contributed to the construction of baptistries distinct from the church where the rest of the community remained at prayer.

Throughout the Middle Ages (from the fifth to the fifteenth centuries), a number of influences contributed to the evolution of Christian churches in the West. A deep respect for the real presence of Christ in the consecrated bread and wine fostered an emotionally charged Eucharistic piety. People felt that they were unworthy of Communion, and they began to receive it less frequently. The highlight of the Mass became the Communion of the priest, not of the faithful. Consequently, the faithful nurtured their piety on the newly inserted elevations of the host and chalice during the Mass, at special ceremonies of Eucharistic exposition and adoration, and in the centralized placement of the tabernacle. Ornate high altars were built in the apses of churches, and these became the focus of worship for the Catholic community.

Side altars appeared in the aisles and to the sides of the apse. These allowed several priests to offer Mass at the same time in an age when concelebration was not practiced.

Gothic architecture had its beginnings in the construction of St. Denis Church just outside Paris (1140–1144). Pointed arches and exterior buttresses sent churches soaring to higher altitudes than ever before. A city's skyline was characterized by its church's profile. Rose windows were enthroned above the doors, and stained glass captured and colored the exterior light. The grand interior space made worshippers feel humble in the presence of God. This design had a profound impact on the history of Christian architecture, and it remains iconic. To this day, many people—Christians and non-Christians alike—think a church looks like a church if it has a rose window and pointed arches.

The Church adapted other styles to its purposes as the history of architecture unfolded: Renaissance, Baroque, Neoclassical, and so forth into the twentieth century. The liturgical renewal promulgated by the Second Vatican Council called the Church back to its early Christian sources, partly to preserve the integrity of its symbols. If ornamentation had been used primarily for decoration, it was redirected to underscore the central purposes of the liturgical action. For example, many churches had been designed to draw one's attention to the tabernacle because it was the center of Catholic devotion. After the Council, this attention shifted to the freestanding altar table because the sacrifice of the cross is made present there, and from there the faithful are fed with the Body and Blood of Christ. Churches became less focused on private devotion and more on public worship.

This caused dramatic changes in the shape of the nave—the space for the assembly. Prior to this time, shaping the nave like a basilica was never seriously questioned. But the shortage of priests gradually called for larger parish churches, electronic sound amplification made the apse unnecessary, and electric lighting supplemented or eliminated the need for natural light from windows. Accessibility for people with disabilities dictated changes in the approach to buildings.

Hence, it is common to see a nave stretch wider than ever before. Seating the faithful around more sides of the altar allows them to be physically nearer the center of activity. Seeing the faces of others, worshippers regain some of the intimacy that characterized the early house churches. In large crowds, a wider nave reminds the faithful that they have gathered not as an audience in a theatre, but as participants at a banquet.

One of the most challenging questions facing Catholic parishes after the Second Vatican Council has been whether to renovate or replace venerable church buildings. Many structures predating the Council emphasized the disparity between the sanctuary and the nave, and between the clergy and the laity. Parishes desiring a more participatory setting for worship engage in long discussions about retrofitting the traditional space for contemporary needs.

Every building is different. Every community is different. Some buildings can be updated very easily, and the community that gathers there can still engage its sacred space as have generations before. But other buildings pose insurmountable challenges. In such cases, the local community needs to discern whether it is better to maintain a building because of its links to the past or to replace it as a service to the future. Such decisions require much prayer, study, and charity.

Questions for Reflection and Discussion

1. What are the main artistic and architectural characteristics that make a church building appropriate for celebrating Catholic liturgy?

2. What are the prominent features of your parish church?

3. How do you interpret those features? What purposes do they serve?

Chapter 3

Serving as a Minister of Liturgical Environment

Liturgy is "the participation of the People of God in the 'work of God.'" . . . Those who respond to God in worship and in service are given the privilege of becoming coworkers in the divine plan.

—*Built of Living Stones*, 19
(See *Catechism of the Catholic Church*, 1069 and 2567)

First Things

Welcome to one of the hidden ministries of the Church! Equipped with humility, open hearts and minds, ladders and fish line, fabrics and flowers, you will do your work when the church is empty. You, your team members, and the Holy Spirit take on the task of creating an environment that draws the faithful more fully into prayer, doing your work while the rest of the community is engaged elsewhere. The planning and preparation you do likely will take more time than actually putting the environment into place. Whatever the stage of your work, starting with prayer is essential if your labor is to bear the desired fruit, which is deeper prayer for those who gather to worship in this space.

As "coworkers in the divine plan"[1] who help worshippers enter more fully into a relationship that transcends time and space, your efforts require firm footing. Whether your prayer is a simple repeated verse or a more elaborate Liturgy of the Word, centering yourself in prayer helps you remember that it is God's holy people you are privileged to serve.

I, through the abundance of your steadfast love,
    will enter your house.
I will bow down toward your holy temple
    in awe of you.

Psalm 5:8, NRSV

Forming a personal and team habit of praying before, during, and after your work will give you humility, move you to consider the ideas of others, and in the consensus that develops, the Spirit will stimulate creativity that results in an environment transcending your personal taste—connecting both you and your community with the eternal.

---

1. BLS, 19; see CCC, 2567.

This esoteric work is usually not done by theologians or philosophers, but by ordinary people, sometimes with little training or background in liturgy. Consider this story of a typical initiation into the ministry of the liturgical environment. Burnout had disbanded a long-lived group of church decorators at a particular parish, and a member of the worship council teamed up with another parishioner to prepare the church for Christmas. A few weeks earlier they had climbed into the crawl space above the church to survey the available materials: the crèche, a couple of ancient artificial Christmas trees, a box of tangled lights, a pair of outdoor wreaths, and a set of intricately appliquéd angel banners. Enlisting more volunteers, they cut down a live tree, bought some evergreen roping and wreaths from the Cub Scouts, poinsettias from the eighth-graders, and took advantage of a sale on lights at a local hobby shop.

Christmas Eve morning, the church was buzzing with activity and hummed carols. Atop a ladder, hanging the floor-to-ceiling banners, one of the new decorators noticed her cochair across the church engaged in a distraught conversation which ended in the abrupt departure of two volunteers. Shaking his head, he made his way toward her. "Blue lights," he said. "Blue lights?" she asked. "To honor Mary. The tree is supposed to have blue lights," he replied. The two had purchased white lights, unaware of the history of the tangled box of lights they'd abandoned. Budget, time, and availability meant that blue lights were not going to shine at St. Regis that Christmas, but the two new decorators recognized the need to address the feelings of the parishioners who interpreted their absence as a slight to the Mother of God.

White lights shone on the parish tree that Christmas, and the statue of Mary was joined in her niche by a statue of Joseph holding the Child Jesus, along with evergreens and poinsettias to honor the Holy Family. That evening, in the midst of a conversation with the upset parishioners in which the new cochairs admitted ignorance and explained their efforts to honor Mary, a tearful gentleman interrupted. "I just have to tell you," he said, "how much it means to me that you used the angel banners this year." His recently deceased wife, Helen, had designed and sewn the banners, but they had not been used for at least five years.

Changes in liturgy, even something as seemingly minor as the color of lights, will evoke emotional responses. No one can intuit the way any given parishioner will interpret changes, but open dialogue helps everyone. During planning stages it's important to ask questions such as "How has the church been decorated in the past for Easter?" or "What do you like best about the church during Christmas Time?" Informally interviewing people of different ages and levels of involvement can yield a wealth of guidance, and most are flattered to be consulted. Conversations begun with such openers as "When I was visiting Our Lady of the Lake last week, I noticed (whatever it is that you noticed and want to implement at your parish). What do you think?" can minimize the reaction when changes are made to longtime customs. They can generate new ideas and increase the membership of your liturgical environment team. As members share the gems mined in these individual exchanges, the Spirit enters in, building consensus that results in liturgical environments that truly draw people to God.

The tools of liturgical environment are tangible items used to communicate intangible beliefs and values. Everyone will not see them in the same way as the liturgical environment committee members, largely because we don't all have the same experiences. Angels at Christmas have a clear scriptural frame of reference, but to Helen's family, they carried a deeper meaning. When someone corners you after Mass to complain, your gut reaction may be, "If they don't like the way we do it, they can find someone else to do the work." Openness to the suggestions of parishioners, even when it comes in the form of venting or criticism, is an important part of every minister's work. Thanking someone for their opinions or saying, "I hadn't thought about it that way," or "I'll share that with the committee," honors the presence of Christ in that individual. As we open our hands and hearts in loving service, the Spirit moves us to communion with each other and with the Trinity. If this already sounds challenging, let's open some possibilities that make the work of the liturgical environment team even more complicated—and fascinating.

A Church of Many Cultures

When speaking to large gatherings, South African Anglican Archbishop Desmond Tutu often invited the crowd to raise their hands, then move their hands, then look at their hands, and see that they are the rainbow people of God. The visual image his words invoke leads to a crucial insight. Because we believe all people are created by God, in God's image and likeness, excluding people of other cultures and races or expecting them to assimilate to the dominant culture is an injustice. It deprives minorities of the hospitality God desires for them, and it also deprives those in the dominant culture of experiencing facets of God they cannot know without experiencing other cultures.

The spiritual essence of the liturgy is by nature welcoming and inclusive—expressing that inclusivity in the prayers, the Scripture, and the Body and Blood offered from the altar. The choices that communities make about other aspects of the liturgy should express that inclusivity also—the music, for example, and the liturgical environment. The images, colors, and symbols that adorn the physical space when your community celebrates Mass can communicate that you are committed to making everyone welcome and to encountering a fuller spectrum of God's identity. Keeping in mind that although most members of your assembly participate physically in the setting, some may have to view the Mass remotely through live streaming or a recording;

ministers of liturgical environment must consider what can be seen by the participants and what signals those visuals are sending.

A 2016 study commissioned by the United States Conference of Catholic Bishops (USCCB) reported that more than 6,300 parishes in the country serve distinct ethnic and cultural groups, and that culturally diverse parishes are the fastest growing nationwide.[2] If your parish is not already culturally and racially diverse, it likely will become so soon. The USCCB offers several resources to assist parishes as they *integrate* cultural diversity.[3] What exactly does integrating culture look like?

Your parish is likely welcoming. Parishioners greet those who enter with smiles and hospitable language and willingly lend a hand, regardless of their race or culture. Just as you would at home, you are delighted to entertain others. However, in parish life, the goal is not to expect parishioners outside the dominant culture to be perpetual guests. In Christ's beloved community, where diversity is valued, the goal is for everyone to participate unreservedly in the ministries, celebrations, and life of the parish.

What do we mean by culture, and what is the role of ministers of liturgical environment in encouraging and nurturing cultural diversity in the parish? The Church defines culture in various ways: culture includes values and ways of expressing beliefs about God. Culture has a language—spoken or otherwise expressed—that voices feelings and ways of living. Culture defines behaviors as proper or improper. Culture includes material aspects such as symbols, foods, clothing, and furnishings in homes.[4]

Ministers of liturgical environment have a unique role to play in creating a church environment where all parishioners and visitors see themselves as part of the family. Look critically at the composition of your committee. How are the cultures and races of your parish represented? Whether your parish is one family or parallel communities that cordially share parish space, could the parish move toward creating liturgical environments that recognize and value everyone? Is it not time to invite and include representatives of your parish's diverse cultures to the table—both as members of the committee and as consultants? A bulletin announcement rarely yields much fruit as a recruitment tool, but it does alert the entire parish of your intent. Personal invitations to conversation are the most effective starting place. Express your genuine desire to listen and learn. Ask parishioners, whether immigrants and newcomers, or

2. Mark Gray, *Cultural Diversity in the Catholic Church in the United States*, The Center for Applied Research in the Apostolate, 2016, https://www.usccb.org/issues-and-action/cultural-diversity/upload/Cultural-Diversity-Summary-Report-October-2016.pdf.

3. The Secretariat of Cultural Diversity in the Church, Fall/Winter Newsletter 2020, *One Church Many Cultures: The Good News of Many Cultures*. https://www.usccb.org/resources/FINAL%2011.17.20%20WEB%20SCDC%20Fall%20Winter%202020%20Newsletter%20final3_0.pdf.

4. See articles about the specific characteristics of the cultures that make up the Church in the United States on the website of the United States Conference of Catholic Bishops, https://www.usccb.org/committees/cultural-diversity-church.

The parish environment for Advent can be integrated with decorations for Simbang Gabi, the Filipino nine-day series of Masses preceding Christmas.

longtime parishioners of different races and ethnicities who have simply never been asked, to share their feelings about liturgical environment. Ask what the decorations in their home churches looked like during seasons and celebrations of the liturgical year. Inquire about feast days and devotions important to them and the customary ways of observing them. Take notes. You're trying to learn about the aesthetic sensibilities of different cultures—about the different colors, symbols, objects, and arrangements through which cultures express festivity, quiet joy, penitence, patient waiting, fortitude, trust, comfort, and so forth. How does each culture create an ambiance for reflection and prayer? Ask about these things before sharing about the current customs of the parish church or the liturgical norms required by the documents.

A single witness is not adequate, of course. Among Latin Americans, there are people from Bolivia, Colombia, Ecuador, El Salvador, Guatemala, Mexico, and Puerto Rico, to name a few, each of whom has "twists" on sacramental celebrations, such as Quinceañeras (a special celebration of a girl's fifteenth birthday) and devotions like *Posadas* or *Via Crucis*. Black Catholics from different regions of the United States may report different ways of celebrating. Immigrants from the African nations of Kenya, Cameroon, Nigeria, and Somalia will have very different stories to tell, as will Native Americans, Vietnamese, Pacific Islanders, Haitians, and Jamaicans. The USCCB offers newsletters and resources for and about African American, Native American, Hispanic/Latino, and Asian/Pacific Islander communities and practices.[5]

---

5. Find them by combining the name of the group with "USCCB" in your search engine.

Looking over some of these resources could help you develop specific questions to ask parishioners. You may also want to consult leaders in nearby parishes who are a step ahead of you in this journey. For some, spoken language may be a barrier to conversation. If translators are available, utilize them. Pictures and drawings might be a viable alternative.

Forming the Team

In addition to seeking out diverse ethnic and racial backgrounds on the liturgical environment team, give thought also to genders and generations. Men and youth are often underrepresented. Although you will likely not be able to attract committed people in all these categories as core members, try to find diverse consultants willing to offer regular feedback and conversation.

Apart from identities, consider the sorts of expertise a team needs. Just as there are many gifts, but one Spirit, so also is there one liturgical environment team with many types of experience and skill. When forming your team, consider the strengths of each member and recruit new members to provide the skills you lack. A core group of three to seven members can determine design, plan and prepare materials, then recruit workers to take on particular tasks. Ideally, someone will serve as a coordinator who will also act as a liaison with the parish staff and the parish liturgy committee. Every member of the team need not have every skill, but every member of the team does need to be open to coordinating skills with others to produce the liturgical environment.

For the core group, knowledge of liturgy, design, art, and architecture, along with a sensitivity to cultural diversity are essential. Communication, organization, and planning skills are also required. A three-year commitment with a rotating membership works well for a core group. If the first year in the group is spent learning, the second year leading, and the third year mentoring the newest members, the core can continue to renew itself. Some members will want to renew their commitment for another three years and others will move on to other ministries. The core group should work together well in advance of the seasons, creating a plan that will be executed by many workers. Set the yearly calendar early, including planning meetings and work days so that members are able to be present as much as possible and volunteers can plan ahead.

What if the expectations and desires of a group of parishioners (whether in the minority or dominant culture) are very different from the prescriptions of Church documents? The team (including the pastor) is, of course, beholden to the teachings and norms of the Church. They would, ideally, try to understand and explain the deeper reasoning behind the norms while at the same time trying to understand the need behind the desire of the group and suggest other ways the need might be met.

What if, after much consultation and research, the team realizes that the cultural aesthetics and expectations of some of the groups are, on some occasions, incompatible? For example, what if one culture's idea of Easter joy is "less is more" while another group's idea is "more is more"? To some extent, such incompatibilities have always been part of community life, which is why disciples are always called to patience and self-sacrifice. That said, these may be opportunities to exercise wisdom and creativity. The team could try to put aside anxiety and consternation and brainstorm some strategies. For example, the groups could graciously take turns—on one occasion exercising patience and self-sacrifice, and on another, seeing their aesthetic desires fulfilled in the environment. Or perhaps the team could come up with a completely new idea that managed to meet the needs of both groups at the same time. Discussions like this demand candor and trust. If over time everyone sees that the team is sincerely committed to finding ways to honor everyone's needs and communicates honestly, it becomes easier to arrive at solutions.

Skills Needed

Aside from the vital skills of group problem-solving and communication already discussed, particular practical skills may be needed for special projects: building trade expertise such as carpentry, electrical expertise, painting, or being able to anchor hooks in brick. Roofers, who have little fear of height, can negotiate high beams easily. Flower arrangers, plant care experts, and those talented in sewing are needed. Others may be skilled in communicating, delegating, and organizing tasks. Still others may be veteran bargain shoppers who are willing to be on the lookout for needed materials.

Communicating the help needed for the liturgical environment clearly and often encourages members of the parish to share their talents. Parishioners of many ages are willing to assist if the tasks are clearly explained and fit with the parishioner's talents. Enlist workers through announcements in the weekly bulletin, newsletters, postings on the parish website, personal invitations, and recruiting at parish talent fairs or stewardship events. Many people are willing to donate two hours on Holy Saturday morning to prepare plants or hang banners for the Easter Vigil. When needs and instructions are clearly stated, when deadlines and budgets are established in advance of work, then the transition from one volunteer to another is smooth and helpers will gladly return for another project.

Knowledge Needed

Knowledge of the Liturgy

The blue-light debacle in the opening story illustrates the importance of knowing the community's customs. But you will need knowledge in another primary area: liturgy is the focus of your work. Beyond the foundation provided in chapter 1 of this book, a good overview of all the liturgical elements that need attention during the current liturgical year can be found in an annual liturgy preparation guide such as *Sourcebook for Sundays, Seasons, and Weekdays: The Almanac for Pastoral Liturgy* (see the resource section). But in addition to such specific publications, you will want to steep yourself in the many aspects of liturgy—the ritual, communal prayer of the Church. Be attentive to the words of the prayers and the Scriptures. Listen carefully to the music. What does the ritual require of the presider and the assembly in terms of posture and verbal participation? How do the furnishings function? What physical elements are needed? Visit other churches during liturgy and note the details of celebration. How is the community immersed in the current liturgical season?

Becoming a student of liturgy will help you become a more effective minister of the liturgical environment. Delving into Scripture is a great place to begin. Lectionary-based study of the Scriptures can be done in a group setting at your parish or individually through various resources (see the resource section). You will also want to devote time to the liturgical documents. It is especially effective to gather with the liturgy team, to read and discuss such documents as *Sacrosanctum concilium* (the *Constitution on the Sacred Liturgy*), the first document written at the Second Vatican Council in 1963, and the *General Instruction of the Roman Missal* (in its most current English translation for use in the dioceses of the United States, 2011). Of special interest to your ministry is the document published in 2000 by the USCCB, *Built of Living Stones: Art, Architecture, and Worship.*[6] For the newcomer to liturgical study, a knowledgeable mentor guiding your discussion and answering questions is important. Your diocesan office of worship can direct you to seasoned ministers of liturgical environment who can assist you. Dioceses often offer workshops and days of reflection for liturgical ministers and information about national organizations, conventions, and publications; make sure you are included on the appropriate mailing lists.

On the webpage of the USCCB (https://www.usccb.org/) you will find much valuable information. From the home page, click on the tab "Prayer and

---

6. The *Constitution on the Sacred Liturgy* and *General Instruction of the Roman Missal* can be found online by entering the title in your search engine. All three documents are included, along with many other documents, in this anthology: *The Liturgy Documents, Volume One*, fifth edition (Chicago: Liturgy Training Publications, 2012).

Worship" and explore the various options. You will find articles on liturgical topics and some of the documents already mentioned. Some of these are issued by the Holy See (Rome), some by the USCCB, and some by the Committee on Divine Worship (formerly known as the Bishops' Committee on the Liturgy, or BCL). You will also find here a link for purchasing the newsletter of the Committee on Divine Worship, which reports on business discussed at meetings of the committee and the progress of various rites and documents making their way through the long process of revision. There is also a link for the official liturgical calendar for the United States, an annual publication. The seasons, memorials, feasts, and solemnities of the Church year are the foundation for the liturgical environment. Other resources to help you track the liturgical year are provided in the resource section of this book. Especially important is the Ordo, the book published annually for each reason that gives the requirements for daily liturgy.[7] You would consult the ordo to learn the liturgical color for a given day.

Make a point of developing a good relationship with the other liturgical ministers and staff at your parish. You will need to interact with these people smoothly and often. Good communication among the ministers of liturgy can prevent mishaps and distractions during liturgies. For example, you will need to ensure that priests and deacons have vesture that permits poised movement, and that they can carry out all the sacred gestures without fear of knocking over the sacred vessels, candles, or floral arrangements. Placement of sacred vessels, books, and other items necessary for liturgy must lend themselves to graceful access.

Sacristans make sure the elements needed for the liturgy are in the appointed places. They can direct you to the Ordo, the *Roman Missal*, the *Lectionary for Mass*, and the *Book of the Gospels* (if your parish uses one)— all of which are important resources for your planning.

Your work could have a positive or negative impact on still other liturgical ministers, so it's important to consider their work. Lectors need to be able to approach the ambo without obstacles blocking their way, and they rely on unobstructed lighting for their ministry. Extraordinary ministers of Holy Communion likewise must navigate space. Discussing with the music director the symbols prominent in the readings for a given season or day can result in musical selections and church adornments that subtly reinforce the season and each other—a wonderful outcome of collaboration. Communicating often helps avoid all sorts of problems. As you can imagine, placing dried materials near an organist prone to hay fever can spell disaster.

Ultimately, the work of the minister of liturgical environment complements that of other ministers toward this end: the celebration is prepared so that it

---

7. *Ordo: Order of Prayer in the Liturgy of the Hours and Celebration of the Eucharist,* published exclusively by Paulist Press in the United States.

"leads to a conscious, active, and full participation of the faithful, namely in body and in mind, a participation fervent with faith, hope and charity."[8]

In all your preparations, the first question to ask should be, "How will this enable the assembly to participate more fully and actively in the liturgy?" Next ask, "What symbols, colors, textures, and fragrances can we use to resonate with the Scriptures, the symbols of the season, the rites, and the music?" Another important question to pose is, "How will we execute this plan so that the liturgical ministers can perform their duties with grace and integrity?"

Knowledge of the Community

Considering the quotation with which this chapter began, it is clear that "the participation of the People of God"[9] is essential in the liturgy. If ministers of the liturgical environment are to use the materials of nature and craft artfully to help the assembly respond to God in worship and in service and so become "coworkers in the divine plan,"[10] they had better understand how the customs and cultures of these people influence the way they read the liturgical environment. The stories and observations already related in the chapter have shown how tricky this is and described some ways the team might deepen their understanding of the people they serve.

Knowledge of the Physical Plant and Resources of the Parish

Mechanical and architectural aspects of your church are of great importance to your work. As the team begins planning, you'll want to learn about locations, policies, and practices related to windows and doors, heat and air conditioning, beams and walls, sinks and water supplies, hooks or hangers on walls or furnishings, ladders and step stools, keys to the church, trash and recycling disposal, cleaning supplies, electrical outlets, and lighting.

Learn how involved the pastor and staff members need to be in your work—who needs to be consulted about which issues and what information various staff members can furnish.

If you don't already know the parish history and customs, you'll need to ask about them: when the church was built, the patron, cultural observances, the significance of artworks and furnishings. You'll need to learn how the church has been decorated for the seasons in the past, about any special needs for weddings and funerals, what decorating materials and supplies the church has and where they're stored, what florists or other suppliers are usually used, and what budget the liturgical environment team is allotted.

---

8. GIRM, 18.
9. BLS, 19; CCC, 1069.
10. BLS, 19; CCC, 2567.

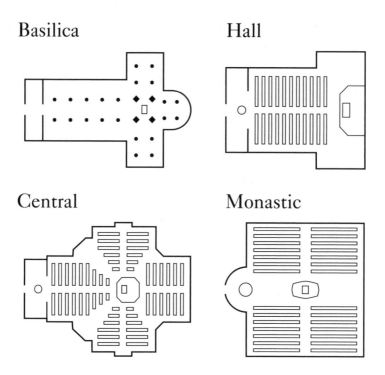

Figure 1. Typical layouts of church building.

Consider Where Your Building Fits in the History of Liturgical Architecture

Recalling the history of the liturgical environment summarized in chapter 2, think about the layout and style of your building. Does it follow the basilica style—a long, narrow rectangle with central aisle leading toward the sanctuary? Does it have transepts? Perhaps the shape of your building is more square, like a large hall, but still with a central aisle leading toward a sanctuary at the far end. Or does your building follow a more central plan in which the nave takes a semicircular shape, with the assembly seated so that all face the sanctuary and multiple aisles lead toward it from the outside? Or is the seating area in your building (or perhaps in the daily Mass chapel) designed in a monastic, antiphonal style: the assembly sitting along two sides of the church with the altar, ambo, and presider's chair placed along an axis in the center?

As you read earlier, at the time a church building is constructed, various factors may guide architectural choices—a favored artistic style, specific liturgical practices, or theological issues. LTP's DVD *A History of the Mass* provides a wonderful visual tour of varied architectural elements in Catholic churches, with catechesis on the Mass. (It may already be available in your parish or diocesan media library.) Another option is an Internet search with the terms "virtual tours" and "Catholic churches"; a quick search will yield many options. What may seem cumbersome in your building today will probably make more sense when viewed in historical context.

What materials are used in the construction and decor of the building? Natural materials such as marble, wood, brick, and stone are favored in many churches, but local availability of resources may necessitate the use of cinderblock, sheetrock, and paint. Your church ceiling may be vaulted or a grid of tiles. Are the windows stained glass? Is the building newly constructed, recently renovated, or is a building campaign in the works to restore or build the current space? The features of your building need to be looked at critically—both from the perspective of aesthetics and of suitability for various aspects of the liturgy. Analyze these characteristics of the building in natural light and in the evening. What parts should be emphasized? What areas would benefit from artful arrangements of fabric or plants?

Knowledge of Design

While formal training in design is not necessary for the members of the liturgical environment team, a basic understanding of design elements and principles is beneficial.

As you prepare the liturgical environment, you'll want to be aware of the visual elements at play in the arrangements you create: the lines, shapes, sizes, colors, textures, and values (lightness or darkness) of the objects you use. These are elements of a visual language that will allow you to create the ambiance and accentuate the signs and symbols that will lead the assembly more deeply into the liturgy of a given season or day.

Certain design principles can guide you in deciding how to arrange the lines, shapes, sizes, colors, textures, and values of the objects with which you adorn the environment. Here are some fundamentals that you need to understand.

LINE

Line is the edge formed when two shapes meet, as well as the direction an arrangement takes. Horizontal lines suggest earthliness while vertical lines draw the eye upward, and can be seen as a metaphor for the divine. Oblique lines suggest movement, and circles suggest a never-ending path, an image of stability and eternity.

COLOR RELATIONSHIPS

It can be helpful to study the relationships among colors by seeing them arranged on a color wheel. The three primary colors—red, yellow, and blue—are the colors that cannot be created from any other colors. The secondary colors—green, orange, and purple—are created by mixing the primary colors. On the color wheel, they are located where their parent colors overlap. (Green

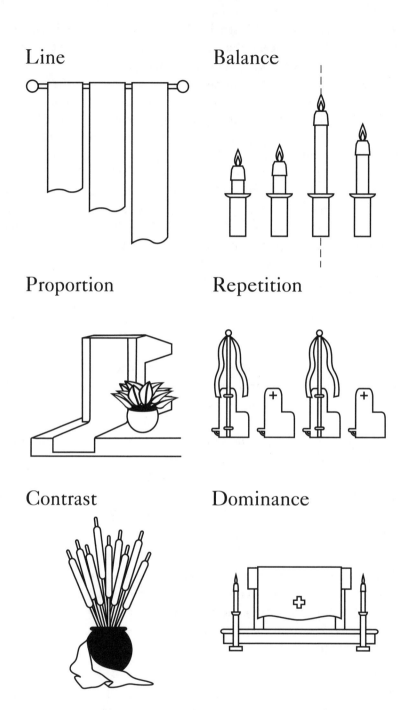

Figure 2. Fundamentals of design.

falls between blue and yellow, orange between yellow and red, purple between red and blue.) The tertiary colors result from mixing a primary and a secondary color: yellow-orange, red-orange, red-purple, blue-purple, blue-green, and yellow-green. The colors directly across from each other on the color wheel are complementary colors, such as red and green, blue and orange, or yellow and purple. When placed side by side, they make each other look brighter. A different effect comes from placing together analogous colors—colors next to each other on the color wheel such as blue-green, green, and yellow-green.

BALANCE

The human eye yearns for balance. Large items can be balanced with small items by using lighter colors for large items, by using more small items in proportion to the large, or by increasing the distance between large and small items. Visualize the center point of the arrangement, and then imagine placing the items on a balancing scale. Judicious use of space helps create balance and impact, so not every inch of the church needs to be adorned. The environment should give an impression of visual balance.

PROPORTION

Proportion guides size choices. A six-foot urn will look harmonious in a church with a twenty-foot ceiling. It will look out of proportion beneath an eight-foot ceiling. A large granite altar placed on a predella (platform) elevated six steps above the assembly requires candlesticks so large that they are likely too heavy to be carried in procession. An eighteen-inch statue of the parish patron is apt to be missed without careful attention to its setting—it will need to be in proportion to the objects around it. Drapes of fabric or ribbon banners need to take into account the height, depth, and width of the space they will occupy.

REPETITION

The repetition of objects reinforces their visual shape as well as their symbolic meaning, but when repetition lacks variety it can become boring. If you are grouping candles as a way of reinforcing the symbol of light, vary the height and circumference of the candles, as well as the holders you use. The rule of threes can be effective in design and in theology. Arranging objects in trios creates a visually pleasing repetition and evokes images of the Trinity.

CONTRAST

Contrast occurs when colors, textures, or directions are juxtaposed. Using shades of colors, balancing horizontal and vertical elements, or choosing colors opposite from each other on the color wheel creates contrast. Crepe fabric matched with burlap can do the same. Even though the liturgy restricts the color choices available to us, natural elements can be used to create contrast.

For example, imagine bright orange lilies set against a background of a regal blue to celebrate the Assumption of Mary.

DOMINANCE

Dominance gives interest to an arrangement. Make sure the dominant element of your design is communicating the dominant message of the season, solemnity, feast, or memorial. The altar is always the dominant feature of a Catholic church. Make sure the environment you plan does not visually obscure the altar as the primary focus for worship.

UNITY

Unity is a primary element for design as well as being a strong value in the Christian community. All of the elements of the environment should be related, creating an effect of unity and coherence. In a very large church, you may want to assign some members of the environment team to take care of the narthex, others the sanctuary, and still others the nave. But planning together ensures unity in the completed work.

Knowledge of Liturgical, Sacred, and Devotional Art

Ministers of the liturgical environment transform church spaces using temporary or transitory art. The materials used and arrangements made are intended to last through a single day, week, or liturgical season, although some items may be carefully stored for repeated use. In spite of the transitory nature of this work, it has a secure place in the tradition of the Church.

Also among the traditions of the Church is sacred art, which may be liturgical or devotional in nature. If these works are already in place at your parish, you will want to be aware of their significance and place in the liturgy.[11] Sacred art reminds us that we are part of the Communion of Saints, that when we gather for Eucharist, we are joined by all members of the Body of Christ. It incorporates images of Christ, Mary, angels, saints, and the Trinity and should be integrated into the design of the church—in

> The tradition of decorating or not decorating the church for liturgical seasons and feasts heightens the awareness of the festive, solemn, or penitential nature of these seasons. Human minds and hearts are stimulated by the sounds, sights, and fragrances of liturgical seasons, which combine to create powerful, lasting impressions of the rich and abundant graces unique to each of the seasons.
>
> —*Built of Living Stones,* 123

stained glass, frescoes, murals, statues, or icons.[12] The crucifix is always the primary artwork in a church and should be honored as such.

While the environment team should not take on the task of repositioning sacred art, you may want to call special attention to particular artworks at various times of the year. Identifying the difference between liturgical art and

---

11. Chapter 3 of BLS provides an in-depth discussion of religious art.
12. BLS, 135.

devotional art is critical if you are to do this well. Statues and icons of the saints and Mary are considered devotional art, as are the Stations of the Cross. You will use elements of liturgical environment to draw attention to these artworks at appropriate times of the liturgical year, but devotional art should never supersede the liturgy. Devotions inspire a piety that flows from and leads to the Eucharist; devotional art should follow the same guideline. Devotional art should not be placed or embellished in such a way that it challenges or obstructs the primary liturgical focal points: the altar, the ambo, the presidential chair, and processional paths.

If the practices regarding devotional art in your parish contradict these principles, be gentle in the transitioning of those practices and enlist the help of your pastor and liturgist. When grandparents in your parish bring their grandchildren to see Baby Jesus in the Christmas crèche that has been displayed in front of the altar since Grandma was a child, and it is no

> **Liturgical arts are integrally related to the sacraments of the Church while devotional arts are designed to enrich the spiritual life of the community and the personal piety of its members.**
>
> —*Built of Living Stones*, 155

longer there, liturgical correctness will not be a selling point. Whether you move the crèche to one side of the sanctuary or form a special niche in the nave or narthex, if you (or others in leadership) have previously done the catechesis to explain that the altar is always the primary focus and have created a reverent and hospitable new place for the crèche, the transition will be less jarring. While the initial change may meet resistance, subsequent changes, such as a change in the placement of the statue of Mary during May, will be smoother.

Designing the liturgical environment, above all, requires attention to liturgical principles.

Knowledge of Symbols

The liturgical environment must be in balance with the religious and devotional art of a community. The symbols and elements of the environment must be dignified and beautiful.

> Churches . . . must be places "suited to sacred celebrations," "dignified," and beautiful.[13] . . . Church buildings and the religious artworks that beautify them are forms of worship themselves and both inspire and reflect the prayer of the community as well as the inner life of grace.[14] Conversely, church buildings and religious artifacts that are trivial, contrived, or lack beauty can detract from the community's liturgy.[15]

---

13. *Rite of Dedication of a Church and an Altar*, chapter 2, number 3.
14. Compare with Pope John Paul II, *Letter to Artists*, 12.
15. BLS, 18.

These elements need not be expensive, and because of the transitory nature of the seasons, prudence should be used in expenditures. At the same time, a budget that appreciates the importance of the liturgical environment to the community's prayer is essential. Dignity and beauty are inherent in the natural world: the variety of grasses and herbs; the textures of stone, wood, and glass; the multiplicity of fruits and vegetables; the grandeur of rivers, lakes, and oceans; the majesty of the stars, the moon, and the sun. Care should be taken to use natural materials whenever possible and practical. The climate of your region will produce natural symbols that speak to you. Harvest in your community may mean pumpkins and wheat, or it may mean oranges and grapefruits. Coral and seashells will suggest water in coastal communities while cattails and native gravel will remind inlanders of rivers and lakes. Using local resources limits the need for artificial symbols, but if, for very good reasons, these are chosen, care must be taken to ensure beauty is preserved.

> Architecture and art become the joint work of the Holy Spirit and the local community, that of preparing human hearts to receive God's word and to enter more fully into communion with God.
>
> —*Built of Living Stones*, 18 (*Catechism of the Catholic Church*, 1098)

During liturgy, symbols take four forms: action, word, images, and music. The postures we assume show our relationship to God and community; the words we pray and music we sing communicate beliefs, emotions, and tone. As ministers of the liturgical environment, you are concerned primarily with images. Attending to the other forms of symbols and consulting with music ministers in particular can reinforce the symbols' power. Whatever symbols are selected for the liturgical environment, they must speak for themselves. As a team, ask, "Will people recognize this symbol and connect it to the season or feast without explanation?" If the team's discussion leans toward the idea of putting together a bulletin insert to "explain" the environment, then the planned symbols are not clear enough to be effective.

The temptation of yielding to personal taste rather than liturgically appropriate style will occasionally arise. Resist the urge to adopt decorating ideas you see in magazines or on television programs. The liturgical environment should transcend secular decorating trends; the time-honored symbols and customs of the Church elevate the art of environment above the trendy; the effect you want is "noble dignity" rather than "chic."

The Work to Be Done

The Church year is a cycle, making the start of each new season the end of an old one. As you prepare for a new season, first take time to organize and care for the items that will be taken down from the current season. Take photos from different angles. Make notes about what worked well, ideas for next year, changes that need to be made, and the cost, placement, and number of plants purchased. Make copies of task lists, invoices, volunteer names, and contact information.

Evaluation

Develop a system for evaluating your work. Beginning with prayer, the team should schedule time to celebrate and evaluate the completed season, perhaps over a simple meal. Invite a member of the parish staff or worship committee to join you; hearing how others perceived your work is useful. Perhaps a neighboring parish or the diocesan offices can recommend an experienced minister who is willing to critique your environment, offering suggestions for improvement. Before the season ends, visit other parishes in your area for ideas, particularly the cathedral. If you see something you want to replicate, make arrangements to talk with the members of the liturgical environment team. Ask for permission to take photos for later reference. Imitation is flattering, and the designers of the plan likely can give you tips. You may even be able to arrange a temporary trade of fabrics, vases, or candlesticks. Put all of this information in a secure file or folder. You will appreciate the reminders next year, and volunteers who come after you will be grateful for the information.

Cleaning, Mending, and Storing

Cleaning and mending tasks such as removing wax from candlesticks or finding someone to repair the broken camel figurine are better done now. Vases and containers that are cleaned before storing will have a longer life. Label materials so they can be accessed easily. Organization is extremely helpful here. When storage closets and cabinets are not available, clear plastic boxes of various sizes can be used.

Planning Ahead

As you begin to plan for the coming year or the next season, (taking time for prayer and reflection on the key Scripture readings, as discussed at the beginning of the chapter), acquaint yourself with the common images and colors used in liturgical environment and art. This chart will be a good reference as you imagine and brainstorm possibilities.

Common Liturgical Images

Light	Candles, crystals
Vegetation	Lily for purity, rose for love, pomegranate for immortality, wheat for Eucharist
Eternity	Green plants/evergreens, circles, triangle
God the Father	cloud, eye, hand

Jesus	Fish, alpha-omega, cross, lamb, Chi-Rho, crown of thorns, light
Holy Spirit	Flames, dove, red
Trinity	Three entwined circles with triangle connecting, shamrock, fleur-de-lis
Evangelists	Quatrefoil, winged man (Matthew), ox (Luke), eagle (John), lion (Mark)
Baptism	Water, scallop shell, white, candle, chrism
Confirmation	Dove, flames, red, chrism
Eucharist	Wheat, grapes/grapevine
Marriage	Entwined rings, white
Holy Orders	Book of the Gospels for deacons, chalice for priest, crosier and ring for bishop, white
Penance	Purple
Anointing of the Sick	Oil of the sick, laying on of hands
Advent	Wreath with four candles: three purple, one pink; O antiphon symbols
Christmas	Crèche, poinsettias, stars, angels, light
Lent	Ashes for Ash Wednesday, purple, cross, Stations of the Cross, desert images
Easter	Lilies, baptismal symbols, eggs, resurrection images
Pentecost	Red, dove, flames
Ordinary Time	Green, symbols taken from Scriptures, seasonal feasts

Liturgical Colors

White	Christmas, Easter, solemnities and feasts of the Lord (except passion), solemnities and feasts of Mary, the angels, saints who are not martyrs, All Saints' Day, marriage, funerals, parish patronal feast, other designated feasts
Red	Passion, solemnities of the Holy Spirit, confirmation, Pentecost, Palm Sunday, martyrdom

Green	Ordinary Time
	If budgets permit, greens can vary: yellow-greens, bright greens, hunter greens, olive greens
Violet	Advent, Lent
	If budgets permit, Advent generally takes on a bluish-purple while Lent calls for a reddish-purple
Gold	Can replace or accent white
Rose	Third Sunday of Advent (Gaudete Sunday) and Fourth Sunday of Lent (Laetare Sunday)
Blue	Not an official liturgical color, but often used in decor as an accent color in the environment for feasts of Mary

This information may help you rough out a running shopping list of possible items to look for throughout the year. Then the day after Christmas, while friends are stocking up on half-price wrapping paper and Christmas cards, the liturgical environment team is digging through 90-percent-off bins at the local craft store in search of silver, gold, red, and white wired ribbon or other items to be used for Triduum and Easter. Before the poinsettias have wilted, the team can be measuring and hemming fabric for Lent. Planning well in advance of a liturgical season allows you to take advantage of seasonal sales and so be good stewards of parish resources. It also helps space out the workload so that volunteers are not overloaded during what are usually busy seasons in families.

Long-range planning of the liturgical environment has several components. First, identify liturgical and secular events of the season, scriptural themes for the season, and special elements, celebrations, or needs of the local community. Planning worksheets similar to these can help focus your work. In this example, Scripture readings are from Year A. To compile the chart of readings, consult the *Lectionary for Mass*.

Liturgical Environment Planning for the Season of Ordinary Time in Summer (Trinity Sunday until Labor Day)

EVENTS	VESTURE COLOR
Sundays of Ordinary Time	Green
Trinity Sunday	White
Corpus Christi	White
Most Sacred Heart of Jesus	White
Nativity of John the Baptist	White

Peter and Paul	Red
Transfiguration	White
Assumption	White

For other civic observances such as Father's Day, Independence Day, or Back to School, simply use the color of the season or day in which they occur.

Scriptural Images

Trinity Sunday	Greet one another with a holy kiss Stiff-necked people Eternal life God is slow to anger, rich in kindness
Corpus Christi	Manna from heaven, bread, cup, living bread, live forever, finest wheat
Peter and Paul	Peter, do you love me? Feed my sheep; the rock
Assumption of the Blessed Virgin Mary	Ark Revelation, 12 stars, clothed with the sun Blessed is the fruit of your womb
Sundays of Ordinary Time	Commandments House built on rock Tax collectors Sinners are loved Harvest is plenty Call of the apostles Speak in light Miracles: healing, nature First fruits A sower went out to sow some seed Weeds among the wheat Pearl of great price Loaves and fishes Peter walking on water Who do you say that I am? Follow me

Next, determine which areas of the church and grounds will be given attention. Having a template that identifies all the sections will enable you to do a quick yes or no depending on the season. Ideally, the entire facility will be fully incorporated, but local weather conditions and resources may require the team to make choices. It is better that some areas be done well than all areas be given hurried or haphazard attention.

Care should be taken to learn and observe the expectations of the Church in regard to decorations around the altar, ambo, and cross. As it is the most important furnishing of the Church, there are specific guidelines regarding the altar. No decorations are placed on the altar; only those items directly required for the celebration of Mass are placed here. Flowers, in moderation, may be placed around the altar except during the season of Lent:

> During Advent the floral decoration of the altar should be marked by a moderation suited to the character of this time of year, without expressing in anticipation the full joy of the Nativity of the Lord. During Lent it is forbidden for the altar to be decorated with flowers. Exceptions, however, are *Laetare* Sunday (Fourth Sunday of Lent), Solemnities, and Feasts. Floral decorations should always show moderation and be arranged around the altar rather than on the altar table.[16]

Restraint should also be used in decorations around the ambo; the ambo itself should not be obscured by decor. The *Roman Missal* notes that the processional cross may be decorated with palm branches on Palm Sunday; at no other time is the cross adorned. If in doubt about the propriety of decorating a particular area of the church, consult your pastor, liturgist, or the *General Instruction of the Roman Missal* (GIRM), especially if you are considering adorning a place that has not been enhanced in the recent past.

Areas for Decoration	Yes	No	Special Date Only
Sanctuary: Areas around the altar, ambo, presider's chair, and cross			
Nave: font, statuary, credence tables, cantor podium			
Chapel of reservation: tabernacle			
Narthex			
Marian garden			
Exterior entrance of church			

---

16. GIRM, 305.

Parking lot

Baptistry

Reconciliation chapel

Other areas

When you have completed this preliminary planning, take time to pray and discuss, developing a common vision within the parameters of the season. In the sample, Ordinary Time, Summer, calls for a simpler environment than the Easter season it follows. The solemnities of Trinity Sunday and Corpus Christi give you the opportunity to gradually simplify after Easter, or you may decide to use the week between Pentecost and Trinity Sunday to make a total transformation. What hues of color will you use? Are there particular banners or images you want to highlight? What floral or plant arrangements do you want to add?[17]

A chart similar to this outlines the plan for the entire season.

Season/Solemnity/Feast	Symbols/Colors/Hues
Ordinary Time, Summer	Green
June	Yellowish green Light/first fruits, green plants with flowers added for special feasts
July	Kelly green Wheat/pearl Nets Continue green plants from June
August	Sage greens with hunter green accents Wheat/harvest/loaves/fishes/first fruits Continue green plants from June and July; add some ripened produce
Trinity Sunday	White/gold, Trinity needlepoint ambo banner, simplify flowers from Easter
Corpus Christi	White/gold, wheat, grapes
Peter and Paul	Red/keys/rock, special flowers added—red?
Assumption	White, fruits, harvest, stars/sun/moon, special flowers—lilies, perhaps blue accent decor

17. Peter Mazar's *To Crown the Year* has some excellent suggestions. (See "Resources.")

Once you have a vision, create simple design sketches. These are easier to do if you first create templates of the areas that you will transform. In your design sketches, pay attention to design elements. How many plants are needed? Where will they be placed? What lengths and widths of fabric in what hue and texture? At what elevations will candles, statues, and floral arrangements be placed? What candle holders will be used for processions and stationary placement? Your vision of the completed environment guides the plan of action while you remain flexible about the final look.

Choosing, Using, and Caring for Materials

Develop and maintain a list of materials and supplies needed in your work. Categorize materials into sections such as fabrics, cloths for the altar and credence table, hardware, florals/plants, ribbons, banners, statuary/icons, vessels, and vestments. (If your parish has multiple priests or deacons, you will need to check all of the choices available.)

Fabrics and Banners

When purchasing fabrics, consider how they will be used. Crepes and lightweight polyester blends drape well, hold color well, and can be easily laundered. Solid color fabrics will be more versatile than patterns; varied textures will give different effects.

When choosing printed or woven fabrics, pay careful attention to the designs. Are the shapes or symbols liturgically appropriate? Will the design distract from liturgy? If you aren't sure, choose something else. Small designs are more adaptable, but larger prints in monotone colors can be used successfully in small doses. Cultural diversity can be honored by the use of batiks, Kenta cloth, or hand-woven fabrics when appropriate.

Draping large quantities of fabric takes practice. First, decide how you will secure the fabric. Split rings sold in the stationary section of stores will slide to allow for easy repositioning, but are sometimes difficult to hide. Lengths of fish line (use a hundred-pound test) can be knotted around the fabric and looped over hooks or nails. The 3M Corporation makes removable strip hangers with adjustable loops, provided you have a smooth surface for securing them. Some churches use drapery rods to suspend the fabric and others provide a pulley system of hooks, but these limit the draping to places where the hardware is secured. Open beams offer space for draping fabric, provided a ladder or scaffolding with sufficient height is available. Choir lofts can be draped as can the fronts of pews. Smaller pieces of fabric can be used to cover plant stands or to create a pooled fabric area for an arrangement of greenery and flowers. Keep in mind these technical details: If the fabric ends will show, they need to be hemmed. Fabric should be pressed and wrinkle-free before hanging.

Banners are often constructed of polyester or cotton blends. When purchasing fabric for these projects, be sure to consult the craftspeople, as the design may dictate the fabrics and trims used. It is helpful to recall what *Built of Living Stones* says about banners:

> Fabric art in the form of processional banners and hangings can be an effective way to convey the spirit of liturgical seasons, especially through the use of color, shape, texture, and symbolic form. The use of images rather than words is more in keeping with this medium.[18]

Because the visual environment you create for the liturgy should not distract from the actions, prayers, and readings in the liturgy itself, it's understandable that imagery would be more appropriate and effective than words on banners. This principle may raise a delicate problem when classes from school or religious education programs help to create the environment, since banners are often the product of craft projects and they often display words. Under no circumstances should children or teens be discouraged from contributing to the liturgy, but the liturgical environment committee may be able to help catechists and teachers steer the children toward images and symbols for their banners.

ALTAR CLOTHS AND COVERINGS

The topmost covering of the altar is always white. During the dedication of a church, the altar is sprinkled with water, anointed with chrism, covered with a white cloth, and surrounded by candles. These symbols of baptism used during the dedication of the altar highlight its importance. It is here—during the consecration of bread and wine—that heaven and earth meet. Following the instruction to dress the altar in white honors its place in liturgy.

> "The beauty and nobility of a vestment should derive from its material and design rather than from lavish ornamentation."
>
> —*Built of Living Stones*, 164 (GIRM, 344)

Altar linens can be purchased from religious suppliers or sewn by parishioners. They may be ornate, lace-trimmed, or simple linen. Coverings of other colors to indicate the liturgical season may be placed under the white cloth. Avoid using commercially designed tablecloths on the altar; using seasonal fabrics from the department store inventory trivializes the importance of this piece of furniture.

VESTMENTS

Although the color of chasuble and stole of the priest and dalmatic of the deacon are dictated by the Ordo, vestments can be purchased from religious suppliers or designed by those skilled in sewing. Many priests and deacons will have their own collection of vestments that should coordinate with the

---

18. BLS, 127.

environment. For special occasions or seasons, the liturgical environment team may want to acquire or produce special vestments.

PLANTS AND FLOWERS

Plants and flowers form a large part of the liturgical environment ministry. Live plants are preferred to artificial. Varieties of green plants such as fern, ivy, bromeliad, schefflera, spathiphyllum, cacti, or palms are good choices for many locales. Keep in mind the natural light your church receives during the day, and then choose plants that are readily available in your area and that require minimal care. Florists or nurseries in your area can help the novice with care instructions. Cleaning the leaves of the plants periodically and treating them with a leaf shine product will extend their beauty.

> The use of living flowers and plants, rather than artificial greens, serves as a reminder of the gift of life God has given to the human community. Planning for plants and flowers should include not only the procurement and placement but also the continuing care needed to sustain living things.
>
> —*Built of Living Stones*, 129

When choosing flowers and flowering plants, remember that the environment has to be sustained for the entirety of the season: for Easter, that means fifty days. Replacing flowers and blooming plants throughout the season is to be expected. Aside from the customary Easter lilies and Christmas poinsettias, other blooming plants can last through a season. During Easter, mums, calla lilies, azaleas, kolanchoe, and bulb flowers such as tulips, daffodils, and crocus provide fragrance and beauty. Work with the floral supplier to make sure plants are just beginning to bloom as you place them in the church. Bulbs can later be planted on the parish grounds to provide beauty during future spring times. Norfolk pines, holly, and cultivated rosemary add interest and fragrance to the Christmas environment. Wood shims can be placed under pots to slightly tilt the plants so that their "faces" are directed forward. Daily Massgoers are often willing to water and trim away dead blooms or leaves during the week; maintaining the plants and florals is a matter of stewardship.

Cut flowers have short lives, but create a wonderful addition to joyous occasions and have an instant impact. Stretch your cut flower budget by employing these tricks: when you purchase the flowers, immediately process them. Trim the ends of the stems at a forty-five-degree angle using a straight blade knife or razor (scissors crush the stem and prevent it from drawing water to the blooms) and strip the leaves from the stem. Next, place the flowers in a bucket of treated water. For each gallon of water, add two tablespoons of chlorine bleach and one tablespoon of clear corn syrup. The bleach will prevent mold and bacteria growth and the sugar will feed the blooms. Leave the flowers for at least two hours (overnight is best) before arranging them.

For those who are novices at floral arrangements, or to stretch the flowers, purchase floral tubes at your local craft supplier. You want the type with a pointed end. Fill the tubes with water, replace the rubber stopper, and place two or three flowers into the tube. Add some greenery such as asparagus fern or baby's breath, then "arrange" the tubes by working them into your potted plants. Compact blooms such as carnations, roses, and daisy mums work well. Another easy way to integrate blooms among your green plants is to arrange tall bud vases, then place them in and among the green plants.

During the fall and winter months, add dried grasses or flowers to the environment by working the stems into the dirt of the plants. Bulletin notices can yield a plethora of dried materials; volunteers can visit the homes of gardeners to harvest them. A quick coating of inexpensive hairspray will seal the dried materials to minimize shedding and the effects upon allergy-prone members of the assembly. Also, ribbon can be judiciously woven through foliage to add interest and color to a season or feast.

Wreaths offer an easy way to work cut flowers into the liturgical environment. Grapevine or other dried wreaths can be wrapped with ribbon and smaller floral tubes can be worked into the wreaths. Place the wreaths on the walls of the church, use them as a base for a green plant, or suspend them from sconces. Small wreaths can be secured with wire to walls to provide interest to fabric draping.

Christmas trees provide a special challenge. The liturgy calls for real rather than artificial vegetation, but fire marshals frown on live trees in public buildings. One call to the local fire department to complain about the fire hazard the tree presents can mean you are forced to dismantle the tree in your narthex on Christmas Eve. Some options to consider: anchor (or plant) a live tree near the church entrance. Most churches will have some exterior electrical outlet; check the location before finalizing the location of the tree. Lights shining in the night announce the season to the neighborhood as well as to arriving parishioners. If you choose to place a live tree indoors, place it in the narthex where it will greet worshippers. When possible, cut down your own tree to assure freshness, place it directly under one of the sprinklers, and be sure it is well watered and fed. Rather than using electrical lights for the tree, consider decorating it with glass crystals or metallic stars that will catch the natural light. If you must yield to using an artificial tree, consider omitting it from your environment. Some parishes use a large fichus tree or Norfolk Island pine during Advent to hang gift tags that parishioners take to purchase gifts for the needy. This tree can be readorned for the Christmas season as a reminder of the generous spirit and service the community shares with others.

Forming a relationship with a local floral wholesaler to supply your plants and flowers will cut costs, even though it means you will need to process and arrange flowers yourself. Check your local adult education programs for classes in floral arranging if no one on the team has this talent. A lavish floral arrangement in the narthex communicates the special quality of a solemnity or feast before folks enter the church. Likewise, arrangements in the sanctuary convey extraordinary occasions.

Often floral arrangements from funerals or weddings are left at the church. Place them amongst the green plants or in places of distinction so that the entire community can enjoy their beauty. As arrangements begin to wilt, rescue the stronger blooms and tube them for an extension of their beauty.

Some parishes have enthusiastic gardeners who maintain a cutting garden on the grounds. These gardens can supply flowers and plant material for the liturgical environment, give beauty to the campus, and be a blessing to the neighborhood— perhaps even a way of drawing people to the church. When planning such a garden,

Be sure that someone is designated to water and care for plants and floral arrangements during the week.

consider your climate and the colors and types of flowers and plants you turn to when creating your liturgical environments through the seasons. A number of parishioners will be willing to offer starts from their own gardens. Contributions and fundraisers could provide funds for buying additional plants. Volunteers could be called to help with weeding and watering.

RIBBONS

Ribbon streamers provide interest and are long-lasting. Placed outdoors to catch the wind, they invite worshippers to enter into the spirit of liturgy as they arrive in the parking lot. Used in processions, they announce a festive occasion. Placed strategically in the nave, they speak of the holiness of God's people gathered for praise.

Whenever possible, purchase your ribbon in spools of fifty yards or more. Florists and crafters can direct you to wholesalers for ribbon, or you can find large quantities in after-holiday sales. Purchase different widths, from one-quarter inch to three inches, in a variety of colors and fabrics. For Pentecost, choose red, orange, gold, or yellow. White and gold can be used to honor the parish patron; add some blue accents to honor Mary. Shades of green will spark enthusiasm during a special Ordinary Time celebration such as the pastor's anniversary. Cut ribbon at an angle to prevent raveling and add interest.

Ribbon can also be used to add interest to green plants, floral arrangements, or trees that landscape the church property. Lengths of ribbon can be wound through the plants, or small bows can be secured to wood floral picks

Figure 3. Two ways to accent a statue with fabric draping.

and placed into the plant's soil. Ribbon looped through sconces or secured to the ambry can enliven the environment.

STATUARY AND ICONS

Statues and icons have long inspired Catholic imagination, young and old. The tradition of placing icons or statues in churches prompts Catholics to learn about and emulate the many paths to holiness; the lives of the saints give hope to us all.

Many parishes have statues and icons that occupy special places within the nave of the church. Images of Mary, Jesus, the Holy Family, St. Joseph, and the parish patron may have permanent homes. Other icons and statues may enhance the parish garden, narthex, school corridors, and chapels. Take an inventory of all the images and statues in your parish and their usual locations. Don't forget the ones that may be packed away, such as the Christmas crèche or some in need of repair. Once you have established an inventory, take time to identify the seasons, solemnities, feasts, and memorials that correspond to each image and note them on your team calendar.

Images with permanent locations can be highlighted on the feasts that honor the holy people they represent. Saints merit special attention during festive seasons such as Christmas and Easter. Fabric draping, plants, or flowers can be placed near or around the images to draw the attention of the faithful. Occasionally, you may want to move a statue or icon to another location as a way of encouraging devotion. With all devotional artworks, take care to keep the attention given to the image in proper perspective to the altar, ambo, and presidential chair. While a statue may be moved to a place of prominence for a devotional prayer service such as a May crowning of Mary, after the service the statue should return to its usual place, or perhaps be relocated to the narthex or chapel. Saints lead us to Christ; no saintly image should obscure or take precedence over Christ during the celebration of Eucharist.

Other statues on your list may be arranged in a more public space for a special feast or observance. Consider placing plants and red ribbons around a statue of the Pietà for the feast of Our Lady of Sorrows. Flowers and fabric draping call attention to a statue of St. Francis of Assisi located in the parish garden when families gather there for a blessing of pets. Spotlights can be installed in a niche or above a suitable shelf in the narthex or other room where people socialize. Rotate images of saints throughout the year to highlight the seasons and provide catechesis about a variety of saints. Stations of the Cross are normally secured to the walls of the church to encourage the faithful to join in the journey that our commitment to the cross requires. Fabric or ribbon can draw attention to the Stations during Lent, but take care to make the effect simple, in keeping with the season. Be especially careful not to obscure the images in the Stations with accents.

Most cultures are devoted to particular saints and feasts. Be alert to collecting statuary and icons of saints dear to the cultural groups in your parish. Native American Catholics may center prayer and activities around St. Kateri Tekakwitha, canonized in 2012 by Pope Benedict XVI. Affectionately known as the Lily of the Mohawks, she was raised by her uncle, a chief in the Mohawk tribe, after her entire family died of smallpox. Her feast day is July 14. Learn about the cause of Nicholas Black Elk, a Lakota catechist, approved by the United States bishops in 2017.

The liturgical environment for *Las Mañanitas* is an important feature of the celebration.

Our Lady of Guadalupe, celebrated on December 12, is an important observance for Hispanics, and really should be for all of us, since she is the patroness of the Americas (South, Central, and North). The celebration often begins before dawn with *Mañanitas*—a serenade to Our Lady—Mass, a reenactment of Mary's apparitions to St. Juan Diego, receptions, and perhaps mariachi bands.

Red roses are an important symbol for this feast, as are images of *la Virgen de Guadalupe*. As this feast is preceded by the Feast of the Immaculate Conception on December 8, efforts to honor both titles of Mary can be easily entwined in your Advent environment, perhaps with floral arrangements combining red roses and white lilies, along with devotional space created for images representing both titles.

Indian Catholics trace their beginnings to the Apostle Thomas, whom they believe brought the Gospel to India. India is unique in that three Catholic rites—all in communion with the pope and all tracing their beginnings to St. Thomas—are active: the Latin rite and two Eastern rite churches (the Syro-Malabar rite and the Syro-Malankara rite). Particularly in southern parts of India, St. Sebastian is a powerful intercessor celebrated with a novena, large parish festivals, and fireworks near his feast day of January 20.

For those who visit and belong to your parish, seeing images of saints who look like them, as well as culturally appropriate images of Jesus and Mary, tells them in an instant that they belong. Saints Monica, Josephine Bakhita, and Father Augustus Tolton (the first Black American priest in the United States), are important in many Black Catholic communities, just as St. Archbishop Oscar Romero is for those who call El Salvador home.

For Tagalog Catholics, devotion to the Black Nazarene, a dark wood image carved in Mexico, clothed in maroon and gold, and brought to the Philippines in 1606, is central. Processions honoring the Black Nazarene (an image of Jesus carrying his cross) occur three times a year, and Christ, in this image, is honored with special prayers each Friday in the Philippines.

CROSSES

Every Catholic church displays a crucifix during the celebration of the Mass. In most churches, the crucifix is a permanent fixture.[19] Processional crosses are not required for liturgy when a crucifix is installed in the church, but they can provide options for exposing the community to culturally and artistically distinct images of Christ. Using different images reinforces the global unity of our Church and validates the experiences of the many members of the parish.

Your parish may own or want to acquire other crosses for special times of the year. A large cross with a stand can be used in the narthex during the season of Lent, or carried in procession as the Stations of the Cross are prayed. A parish garden may be enhanced by the inclusion of a stone cross that withstands the effects of weather. For Good Friday, if it is practical, the large crucifix can be brought down to the level of the people, or another large cross may be used. Although a second or third cross may be used if pastoral reasons suggest that a great many people be given the opportunity for individual adoration, a single cross is preferred.

---

19. BLS, 91, with its note to GIRM, 122.

CANDLES

Candles represent the light of Christ and are always used during liturgy. Purchase quality candles from a religious supplier. These will burn more slowly and cleanly than those available for home use. Brass candle followers help candles burn evenly; bobeches protect floors (and servers' hands) from dripping wax. Inventory the types and number of candle holders in your parish. Candles that must be carried gracefully in procession need to be secured in holders that lend themselves to processions and to safety. Keep the age and size of your altar servers in mind, as they will be the ones carrying the candles. Stands should be located so that nearby plants, fabrics, or ribbons do not cause a fire hazard, and they should be accessible so that candle bearers can easily place their candles in the stands.

Votive candles, candles for the tabernacle, benediction candelabras, and dedication candles require attention and maintenance. Votive candle holders should be cleaned on a regular basis and checked for cracks or chips. Avoid placing a new candle on top of a partially burned candle as this can cause overheating and become a fire hazard.

Candle holders need frequent cleaning to keep wax from building up. A hair dryer can help melt the wax.

Dedication candles are placed in at least four or as many as twelve places on the walls of the church. These candles mark the places the walls of the church were anointed during the dedication ceremony. The anniversary of the church's dedication is an appropriate time to light these candles, as well as other special occasions. When you plan to use the dedication candles, you may want to call attention to their special status with floral wreaths, ribbon streamers, or fabric.

The paschal candle, as "the pre-eminent symbol of the light of Christ,"[20] should be large, beautiful, and new each year. It is possible to make your own, with the advice of someone skilled in candle craft. The candle itself is white; the symbols on it may be in decorative colors. Some parishes purchase a plain candle that can be painted by a talented parishioner (acrylic paints work well). If you do this, be sure to provide instructions about the symbols to be used and request sketches from the artist for review before the actual painting is done. Symbols and colors that evoke scriptural images of baptism (many of which are found in the readings of the Easter Vigil) are especially appropriate. Pre-decorated candles can be purchased from a variety of sources, either in standard sizes or custom made. When selecting a candle, consider the available

---

20. BLS, 94.

paschal candle stand. The height and circumference of the candle should be in proportion to the stand. Consider also the weight of the candle, because during the Easter Vigil, the candle will be carried in procession. The paschal candle will represent the Light of Christ, not only during the Easter season, but at celebrations of baptism and funerals throughout the year, so it must be large enough to bear that symbolism through many hours of burning. It should be obvious to all that this candle is the dominant candle in the church, but it should be in proportion to the size of your building and community. Be sure to budget for the expense of a new paschal candle each year. At the end of the year, the candle could be donated to a mission parish, broken and used as starter for the Easter fire, or some suppliers will offer a discount on a new candle when the old is returned for recycling of the unused wax.

VESSELS

The GIRM gives particular attention to the types of vessels that may be used for liturgy. The chalice, paten, ciborium, pyx, and monstrance must be made of precious metals or other precious materials such as ebony. The materials used cannot easily break or deteriorate. The design may vary according to the "customs of each region" provided the vessel is suited for its liturgical use and is "clearly distinguishable" from vessels used in households.[21]

Pitchers for unconsecrated wine, cruets for water, and vessels needed for ritual hand washing should complement the chalice, cups, and paten, but should be simply designed so they are not mistaken for the sacred vessels.

RITUAL BOOKS

Liturgical books warrant size and coverings that convey their noble role in the sacred work of liturgy. The *Lectionary for Mass*, the *Book of the Gospels*, the *Roman Missal*, the *Book of Blessings,* and other ritual books such as those used for funeral rites or baptisms are usually bound with materials that communicate their importance. Whenever the presider or other ministers of the liturgy require unpublished materials—perhaps a homily text, universal prayer or prayers of the faithful, or a localized blessing—the papers should be secured in a binder or folder. Simple black binders can be used, or ceremonial binders can be purchased in liturgical colors from various suppliers. A talented crafter in your parish may be able to cover binders with fabrics that complement banners or vestments.

---

21. GIRM, 332.

INCENSE

Incense, its scent and smoke representing the prayers of God's people rising up to heaven, is used at funerals, the dedication of a church, during benediction, and at many other liturgical events. Pastoral preference generally dictates the optional use of incense. The containers in which the incense is burned (on charcoal) are known as censers or thuribles. The incense is kept in a boat with a small spoon used by the presider to place the grains of incense onto the burning coals. These containers may be simple earthenware bowls or ornate containers fashioned of brass, silver, or gold. Open bowls of incense may be carried in procession; earthenware pots with numerous openings that are sold at garden centers work well. Cat litter can be used as a lightweight, fireproof foundation for the burning coals that insulates the container so that it can be carried safely. Line the container with aluminum foil before adding an inch or more of cat litter. Budget amply for incense; the cleanest burning pure incense is costly, but is well worth the expense as it provides a longer-lasting perfume. Less expensive incense often contains fillers that cause the irritation resulting in a coughing congregation. Try different fragrances for different occasions. The perfume of Easter can be a floral while the senses at a funeral celebration savor a spicier fragrance.

HARDWARE AND TOOLS

A well-stocked toolbox is indispensable when producing the liturgical environment. Having the needed supplies stocked nearby saves time-consuming trips to the hardware store during setup sessions. Your toolbox should be stocked with these items: hammers (tack hammer, claw hammer, and rubber mallet); screwdrivers in various sizes (flat-blade, Phillips of various sizes); level; awl; superglue; poxy; tacky glue; wood glue; tapes (duct tape in various colors; electrical tape; masking tape; double-stick tape; scotch tape); pliers; wire cutters; drill with various bits; extension cords of various lengths and colors; wire of various gauges; cutting tools (paring knives, box cutters, razor blades, and utility knives); scissors of various sizes; pinking shears; fish line (one-hundred-pound test) drapery weights; safety pins; straight pins; T-shaped pins; staplers; staple guns with various sized staples; nails; screws; cup hooks; swivel hooks; other fasteners; bolts and nuts of various sizes; picture hanging materials; floral tape; bowl tape; floral tubes and picks; floral foam—dry and wet; string, twine, and cord; putty knives and scrapers; steel wool; rubber bands; wood shims; tape measure; ruler; yardstick; cleaners (glass cleaner, wood polish, gum remover, cleanser, metal cleaners, spot cleaners for carpet and upholstery—check with the parish maintenance staff for the correct products); broom and dustpan; vacuum cleaner (standard and portable); mop; trash bags; small saw; and clippers.

Practical Requirements of the Seasons

Advent

The liturgical year begins with a season of hope, expectancy, and preparation, recalling the Hebrew experience of waiting for the Messiah and foretelling the second coming of Christ. Advent's color is violet—a purple favoring blue—which reflects the royalty of Jesus as the Messiah King. The Advent wreath is commonly used during this season. Make sure yours is of substantial size, proportionate to your space, but not so large as to overshadow the altar. If evergreens are not indigenous to your region, consider constructing your wreath of other greenery such as seeded eucalyptus or cacti applied to a wreath form. Real plants are preferable to plastic greenery. Think about suspending the Advent wreath over the central aisle of the nave; if you decide to do this, check with an experienced construction person to assure safe mounting. Hooks or rings can be discretely placed in the ceiling so that they do not have to be removed each year. Locate a ladder of appropriate height so that suspended candles can be lit, arrange a pulley system for lowering the wreath, or you may group the candles on the floor of the nave beneath the suspended wreath.

The Scriptures for Advent draw heavily on God's faithfulness, Mary's willing participation in God's plan, the coming of the Messiah as Mary's child, the prophetic voice of John the Baptist, and the coming of the Lord at the end of time. Beginning four Sundays before Christmas, the First Sunday of Advent follows the solemnity of Christ the King. Within the Advent season, the solemnity of the Immaculate Conception (December 8), the feast of Our Lady of Guadalupe (December 12), and the memorials of St. Francis Xavier (December 3), St. Ambrose (December 7), St. Lucy (December 13), and St. John of the Cross (December 14) are celebrated. The Immaculate Conception, Our Lady of Guadalupe, St. Ambrose, and St. John of the Cross call for white vesture; St. Lucy calls for red. If these are celebrations of special importance in your parish, you may want to add ribbons of the designated color to your plants for those days.

The collection for the retirement fund of religious is taken up on the second Sunday of Advent. Photos of religious men and women who have served your community might be displayed in the narthex as a reminder of their faithful answer to God's call to service. Gaudete Sunday (the Third Sunday of Advent) allows rose vestments in place of violet. Consider placing some pink roses among the greens of the Advent wreath and other greenery for this week or adding some rose-colored ribbon to the arrangements.

In some years, the Fourth Sunday of Advent will become Christmas Eve at sundown. Plan your environment to allow for an easy transition. Gradual additions to your environment during Advent can build toward the Christmas glory.

Christmas Time

The official start of the season is the vigil of the solemnity of the Nativity of the Lord. Celebrating the incarnation calls for a joyful environment, using white and gold, filled with familiar images. Poinsettias and evergreen roping are often used; don't be afraid to introduce unexpected plants and florals such as amaryllis or lilies, which represent Mary, during this season. Gold or pearl lengths of beads can be woven among the plants, hung with ribbon above the font or at the head of aisles. Light-catching crystals or candles suspended overhead reflect light at different times of day. Symbols of Christ drawn from the O Antiphons of the last week of Advent can easily transition to Christmas.

The incarnation celebrates the union of God and humanity; whatever decor you choose, it should allow for the practical needs of the assembly during this season. Remember that churches often overfill for Christmas Masses; for some people, it is one of the few times they visit a church during the year. Welcome all by leaving ample room in aisles and other places of movement for the traffic flow. Learn the requirements of the fire marshal for your building and ask how the parish will accommodate extra worshippers. Is it permissible to set up extra chairs in some parts of the church? Will the overflow crowd be seated in an adjacent space and live video feed be provided of the liturgy in the church? Any of these arrangements will affect the liturgical environment you are preparing.

The Christmas crèche is a devotional element of the environment. Place it in a designated area of the gathering space, in a niche or corner, at the end of an aisle, or in a devotional chapel where people can easily gather before and after Mass. Christmas trees placed outside the church doors, luminaries, and lights strung in trees on the parish property welcome the faithful and catechize the neighborhood.

The Christmas season is packed with solemnities, feasts, and memorials, including the feasts of St. Stephen (December 26), St. John the Apostle (December 27), the Holy Innocents (December 28), and the Holy Family (celebrated the Sunday following Christmas). The solemnity of Epiphany is traditionally celebrated January 6 and ritually celebrated the Sunday after the solemnity of Mary, the Mother of God (January 1). Christmas officially concludes with the feast of the Baptism of the Lord, marking the beginning of Jesus' public ministry.

In some places, parishioners are invited to make donations for Christmas flowers, sometimes in memory or honor of loved ones. As you dismantle the Christmas environment, invite them to take home poinsettias or other blooming plants. In colder climates, provide some plastic bags for safer travel.

Ordinary Time, Winter

Ordinary Time calls for green vestments and decor. During the winter months, choose darker greens such as hunter or spruce. A simpler environment marks the transition from Christmas. Draw your cues from nature in your region. Dried arrangements of grasses and perennial green plants form the basis of your environment during this season, with occasional supplements of fresh flowers provided by weddings and funerals, or added to mark feasts of local importance.

The feast of the Presentation (Candlemas) is February 2. On this day, candles for prayer use in homes are traditionally blessed. Whether you invite parishioners to bring their own or provide simple candles for them, add an abundance of candles to your environment for this day. Ordinary Time celebrates the memorials and feasts of many saints. Consult a liturgical calendar and mark those important locally with special flowers, fabric, or ribbon. Be attentive to the length of Ordinary Time when planning for the season. In some years, it lasts only a few weeks.

Lent

Lent begins with Ash Wednesday and concludes just before the Mass of the Lord's Supper on Holy Thursday. We say that Lent lasts forty days, a parallel to Jesus' time in the desert, but the count is not exact. Ash Wednesday to Holy Thursday is actually forty-four days. This season of conversion and repentance, anticipating the passion and death of Jesus Christ, and also reminding us of our baptisms, uses violet that is a reddish purple, reminding us of the blood shed on our behalf in Jesus' passion and death. A tone of solemn austerity guides the liturgical environment, but there should be enough decor to provide a contrast to the barrenness that Good Friday demands.

Those preparing to enter the Church at Easter, the elect, are engaged in intensive preparation during Lent. The assembly may be participating in some rituals such as the scrutinies on the Third, Fourth, and Fifth Sundays of Lent, and there may be other rituals outside of Sunday Mass that call for simple additions to or rearrangement of the environment; check with your liturgist or priest.

Palm Sunday (or Passion Sunday) is the last Sunday of Lent, marking the entrance of Jesus into Jerusalem amid the waving of palms and "Hosannas!" Vestments for Palm Sunday are red; integrate red into your existing Lenten environment. Lavish use of palms in all shapes and sizes can point toward the Triduum that will be observed in a few days. Consider placing palm branches near or around the baptismal font, ambry, and throughout the nave. Those gathered for Palm Sunday's liturgy will carry palms in procession. You may want to order some red kalanchoes or other small flowering plants to use on

Palm Sunday, then remove them for use again on Holy Thursday, and finally in your Easter environment.

The Sacred Paschal Triduum

These Three Days that mark the transition from Lent to Easter are the most sacred days of the liturgical year as they recall the Paschal Mystery in solemn yet splendid ritual. The Triduum demands much of the liturgical environment team, as each day calls for special treatment.

Holy Thursday's color is white. The parish Mass is generally celebrated in the evening. The diocesan Chrism Mass at the cathedral will have been celebrated earlier in the day if not earlier in the week. As the Church recalls the institution of the Eucharist and the priesthood, she also recalls the washing of the feet and the service that is required of all disciples of Jesus. At the end of Mass, the Eucharist is carried in procession from the church to an altar of repose—usually in a chapel—for adoration.

At the end of the Mass of the Lord's Supper on Holy Thursday, the church is stripped and prepared for Good Friday. Keep this in mind as you plan your environment. Choose plants and candles that can be easily carried in procession from the church to the adoration chapel. Determine how the ritual of washing feet will be managed; will people approach the priest who is situated in a stationary place, or will the priest and his servers travel from person to person? Where will the basin, pitcher, and towels be placed? How will the pitcher be refilled? Where and how will chairs or stools be placed? Be sure to leave ample room for graceful movement during this important ritual, and make sure the foot washing is located where it will be visible to the assembly.

The bread and wine used for Holy Thursday deserve special attention. This may be the one time a year that parishioners bake the bread for Mass, or a wine is used that looks or tastes different than the one to which the parish is accustomed. If a more festive chalice and paten are available, use them for this occasion. Using more formal vessels heightens the awareness of the faithful that this is a special night.

Your parish may have a separate adoration chapel. If not, a place should be designated for the reservation and adoration of the Eucharist through the evening. In preparing the place where the procession will end, remember that a large number of people will gather at first, until only a few remain when the concluding prayers are offered. Simple placements of candles, plants, and fabric will help communicate the importance of this vigil.

On Good Friday, Mass is not celebrated. The principal service is the celebration of the Lord's Passion, which includes the proclamation of the passion, the adoration of the cross, special prayers, and a Communion service. Stations of the Cross may be prayed at other times on this day.

For Good Friday, all plants are removed. Vigil candles are removed or covered; the altar is bare. The vestments for the priest are red and the fabric used to cover or veil the cross is violet. During the Good Friday service, if the crucifix or cross is not brought up the aisle, it will be uncovered in the sanctuary. This means you will have designed a way to cover the cross that permits easy removal. Strips of fabric can be strategically placed to allow for sequential removal; the removal will need to be practiced in advance by the servers, particularly if the crucifix or cross is suspended above them.

Candles and a simple altar cloth and corporal will be brought to the altar in preparation for Communion, and will be removed following that simple service.

Tempting as it may be to begin the Easter decorating after the last Good Friday services, honor this day by leaving the church totally unadorned and by taking reflective time for yourself. Plan to begin the decorating work following Morning Prayer on Saturday.

Holy Saturday

Holy Saturday is the final day of preparation for elect and candidates. Following Morning Prayer, they may

Plan well ahead of the season so you can make the necessary changes easily when the time comes.

participate in the ephphatha rite or the choosing of a baptismal name. Be aware that you may be sharing the space with them as you go about your respective preparation for the Easter Vigil.

Easter celebrates the resurrection of Jesus, who redeemed the human race. This glorious season, filled with alleluias, begins with the Easter Vigil. Use white and gold or silver abundantly; accents of blue can call to mind the waters of baptism. Fill the church with the scent of spring flowers: lilies of different varieties, tulips, kalanchoes, daffodils, or hyacinths. This is the time of year to invest in new green plants; nestle ivies and flowering plants together in baskets. The symbols of baptism—through which we enter into life with Christ—should be accented. Use flowers and plants to highlight the font, but be sure it can be easily accessed for the baptisms that will be celebrated during the Easter Vigil. Ribbons suspended above or banners behind the font call attention to its role in this season. The ambry, where the sacred oils are housed, deserves some attention, and the stand for the paschal candle can be decorated with flowers. Consider a small wreath of fresh flowers around the candle holder (for more about the paschal candle, see page 53).

The Easter Vigil starts with a ceremonial fire outdoors, from which the Easter candle is lit. Braziers for the purpose of containing the Easter fire can be purchased, or if your community permits, you can solicit skilled campers or scouts to prepare the fire. From the Easter candle, the light is shared with everyone in the assembly as they process with small candles to their places in the church. Processional candles can be purchased with wind guards or with cardboard disks to protect hands from melting wax. Place the candles in baskets for easy distribution as people gather, and provide containers in each pew for extinguished candles to protect upholstery from wax drippings.

How will the baptisms celebrated this night occur? By immersion or pouring? Immersion baptisms require lots of large towels for the newly baptized as they emerge from the font. It's also prudent to provide a pathway of slip-proof plastic runners or rugs to prevent slipping on hard surface floors or soaking of carpet. Have extra towels on hand to wipe up puddles.

The Easter Vigil can last as long as three or more hours. Be sure your environment allows for all of the processions that take place during the Vigil, including the procession of the assembly into the church from the fire and the various movements related to the initiations. Especially take into account the number of people who will be baptized and confirmed, their sponsors, and family members, ensuring that they can move easily as the initiations proceed.

Easter Time

Easter lasts for fifty days. Be sure to budget for a new round of flowers midway through the season as the blooms on the initial set of plants will fade. The last celebration of Easter Time is the solemnity of Pentecost, which calls for red vesture. For Pentecost Vigil and Sunday, you will transform the church. Red fabrics, symbols of flame and wind, are all part of the Pentecost experience.

Red and metallic gold ribbons strung with bells and tied to rings can be mounted on banner poles and carried in procession, or placed outside the doors of the church where wind can blow the ribbon as it greets those arriving for prayer. Take out the Easter flowers, polish and trim the green plants, and add some red carnations or roses to the plants, providing a clear contrast to the prior season.

Ordinary Time in Late Spring, Summer, and Fall

Ordinary Time in late spring begins with Trinity Sunday and Corpus Christi. As you bring out the green fabrics and simplify the environment, consider a palette of greens that reflects nature in your region. In early spring, use the yellow-green of new grass emerging, and then move to the shamrock greens

A place for remembering the faithful departed can be created for the month of November.

of summer plants. As fall approaches, consider the golden-greens of fields ready for harvest. Ordinary Time includes the solemnity of the Assumption, the feast of the Transfiguration, and the feast of the Exaltation of the Cross, the solemnity of All Saints, the Commemoration of All the Faithful Departed (All Souls), and it concludes with the solemnity of Christ the King. Highlight these special observances by changing fabrics, adding flowers, or simply creating different groupings of green plants.

Throughout the month of November, the Church remembers in a special way those who have "gone before us marked with the sign of faith."[22] A book bearing the names of the deceased members of the parish may be displayed near the font, along with the paschal candle. Some parishes invite people to bring photos of their departed loved ones to display on a table somewhere in the church. If that is the custom in your community, give thought to how you might prepare and decorate this space. At All Souls' Day Masses, consider placing and lighting extra candles in the sanctuary representing the departed. Family members of those who have died during the year could be invited to take one of the candles home after the Mass.

For the Mexican American community, remembrance of the beloved dead centers around *Día de Muertos*—the Day of the Dead. Whereas All Souls' Day can be sorrowful for Americans of European ancestry, *Día de Muertos* has a touch of festivity about it. In Mexico the family would take a picnic to the graves of loved ones and would feel a sense of reunion and joy. Even if Mexican families cannot celebrate exactly the way they would in Mexico, many features

22. See Eucharistic Prayer II.

of the observance continue, such as certain foods and confections. By now most European Americans are aware of the sugar candies in the shape of skulls eaten at this time of year. In the parish, Mexican families take a different approach to decorating the space for photos of the departed. Instead of somber violet, they will use bright oranges and bouquets of marigolds. In some parishes, parishioners of European descent may be able to adapt and embrace this idea so that the parish can share one large shrine for the faithful departed. Step by step, with much conversation and feeling your way, you may be able to help negotiate more and more adaptation and sharing—on both sides.

Practical Requirements of Particular Rites

Eucharist

The celebration of Eucharist is the source and summit of the Christian life.[23] As the primary worship service of the Church, the Eucharist remains constant as the liturgical year progresses. Preparations for the liturgical environment of a church are always attentive to four locations that are critical in the celebration: the altar, where at the words of consecration the bread and wine become the Body and Blood of Christ; the ambo, where the Word of God is proclaimed and preached; the nave, where the assembly gathers as members of the Body of Christ; and the presidential chair, where the priest leads the Body of Christ in the sacred mystery of Eucharist.

Because the Eucharist is the central shared experience of parish life, consider creating a way to extend the liturgical environment of the Mass to those in your parish who are unable to physically join the community for worship due to health or advanced age. Think about preparing small floral arrangements mimicking those in the church, particularly during the Advent, Christmas, and Easter seasons. People bringing Holy Communion to the home bound can deliver the arrangements as a sign of the community's prayer and care for all its members. You might recruit school children, adult prayer group members, or confirmation candidates to make the arrangements as a service project.

Rites of Initiation

Baptism, confirmation, and first Communion are celebrated together at the Easter Vigil when the elect are baptized. Candidates for reception into the Catholic Church (who are already baptized) may be received on another occasion. In many parishes, first Communion celebrations are scheduled during Easter Time. Baptisms of infants occur throughout the year, and while confirmation is ideally celebrated at Pentecost, the practical considerations of the bishop's schedule dictate the calendaring of the celebrations.

---

23. "The liturgy is the summit toward which the activity of the Church is directed; at the same time it is the fount from which all the Church's power flows" (*Sacrosanctum concilium*, 10).

Whenever baptism, confirmation, first Communion, or reception into the Church is celebrated, the symbols of initiation should be accented. For these occasions occurring outside of the Easter Vigil, prepare an easy-to-implement a plan that can be put into place by sacristans or servers. For baptism and first Communion, the Easter candle is lit and the color white can be integrated, whatever the current season.

For confirmation, the primary color is red. Perhaps a ribbon banner is prepared and placed by the font and ambry, or special coverings for the altar and ambo are used. A special place can be prepared to display the sacred chrism at confirmation, such as a small pedestal table or a short statuary column with a simple strip of red fabric. If confirmation in your diocese is celebrated with middle-school or older students, consider using some ribbon banners on poles to be carried in procession and placed about the nave to add festivity to this sacred ritual.

Try to learn about specific cultural practices around sacraments. Appeal to those in your parish who prepare families for the sacraments of baptism, confirmation, first Communion, first reconciliation, and marriage for help eliciting and sharing information to assist you in preparing for these special celebrations. In many Hispanic communities, each child lights a candle at first Communion, symbolically making the connection with baptism. Parents may ask for prayers of thanksgiving and blessing for a newborn (*Las Presentaciones*) as a precursor to baptism.

Among African cultures, the moment after the Trinitarian formula and pouring of water concludes, the family raises their voices joyfully with trilling and cheers. Many cultures express their joy in more exuberant ways than do European Americans, so leaving room around your baptismal font for movement is one way to welcome these practices. Some bring their child before a statue of the Blessed Mother following the baptism to offer a prayer; making space near the statue for offerings of flowers honors the custom.

Wearing traditional sacramental colors—red for confirmation, white for first Communion and baptism—is common in many communities. While many brides wear white, some will choose colors traditional to their culture: red, gold, green, yellow, or even black. Knowing this information helps you in planning for liturgical seasons: while keeping with the colors of the liturgical year and seasons, you can be sensitive to the variations of colors that may appear in photographs.

Penance or Reconciliation

The Rite of Penance may be celebrated individually in a reconciliation room or confessional. In a larger space, there may be an area for a plant, simple fabric hanging, or artwork that reflects the healing mercy of God. Violet, the color of penitence, is associated with this sacrament. It is not necessary to decorate the reconciliation room with the seasons; the unvarying use of violet reflects the steadfast love of God for us, even as we sin.

Penance services with opportunity for individual confession and absolution usually occur during Advent and Lent, and they call for a transformation of the nave. The additional priests who will hear individual confessions will need spaces that afford privacy, because most churches do not have multiple confessionals or reconciliation rooms. Ponder the configuration of your nave. Space will be needed for those who gather to pray communally, as well as for individual celebrations of the sacrament of penance. Determine how many priests will be available, and then choose spaces for their stations. Two chairs or space at the end of a pew for the priest and the penitent can be marked with a candle. Particularly if the service is in the evening, the lit candles will make the stations easy to recognize. If you do not have an adequate number of candlesticks, use small tables or stands covered with a piece of violet cloth on which you place a large candle, or a grouping of votive candles. Instead of candles, you could use banner poles with simple purple ribbons or a narrow strip of fabric to mark the location of each confessor.

Marriage

Weddings can be among the most challenging situations for the liturgical environment team. If your parish does not have a standing policy for environment considerations for the celebration of the sacrament of matrimony, work with your pastor, liturgist, and worship committee to develop one. Brides and their planners often want to remove elements of the environment because they "clash" with the wedding palette. This sacrament, however, is celebrated within the context of the faith community; the church building and seasonal decor represent the community that will support this couple in prayer and action throughout their marriage. Major changes in the environment to accommodate a wedding should be discouraged; you may even decide that some changes are prohibited.

Make sure those who meet with engaged couples remind them of the liturgical season in which they will be married; the colors of the Church year are standard and couples who are reminded of this will not be surprised when they arrive at the church to set up for the wedding.

Marriage is a sacred and joyful celebration. Candelabras, banner poles, and other festive elements in the liturgical environment cupboard can be offered for the couple's use. Suggest a meeting with the couple well in advance of the wedding to talk over how the church will be decorated at the time of their ceremony and what options are available for personalizing the space. Perhaps the flowers and other decorations brought in for the wedding can be enjoyed and used for other parish celebrations, if the families do not wish to take them away. If very many weddings are celebrated at your parish, however, you may not wish to be responsible for disposing of them. Have responses and suggestions prepared concerning a unity candle, flowers for the Blessed Virgin, pew bows, candles, and other items that might be locally or culturally common.

This is a special time for the couple, and sometimes an anxious time. The tone of your interactions with them could impact their future with the Church. Be flexible and welcoming in your conversations. They may not understand the reasons behind parts of the wedding liturgy, and they may not see the liturgical environment as a sign of the community. Use this as an opportunity to catechize, but not to alienate.

Many cultures have specific wedding customs. For example, the wedding Lazo (Order of Christian Matrimony, 67B) and Arras (OCM, 71B) are so common during the celebration of matrimony in Latino, Filipino, and Mexican families that they officially appear in the newest edition of the *Order of Christian Matrimony*.

Holy Orders

The sacrament of holy orders is usually celebrated at the cathedral as a diocesan event. The ritual calls for particular postures and symbols. If you are in a cathedral parish, the chancery offices will provide the direction and resources the rites require. The ordination of a parish son, however, is often followed by a first Mass at the parish church. Ordinations can happen at any time of the year, but are frequently scheduled to coincide with the conclusion of school semesters. Whether it is Advent, Easter, or Ordinary Time, the regular environment should be brought up a notch or two to honor the joy the occasion merits. Banners, additional flowers or plants, extra candles, and integration of white and gold into the environment are all appropriate.

As with a wedding, meet with the man to be ordained and his family, and consult with diocesan offices before finalizing your plans for the environment. The integrity of the parish decor should be maintained while incorporating symbols and ideas of the candidate for ordination. Clarify expectations about the budget and who is paying for what. Discuss any regional or cultural customs. Suggest using blooms in the floral arrangements that are reminiscent of those used at his parents' wedding, those that are symbolic of a favorite saint, or that are similar to those being used for reception centerpieces as a way of personalizing the celebration.

Anointing of the Sick

As with communal celebrations of penance, parish celebrations of the anointing of the sick call for simple but distinct treatment. You may want to consider using banners symbolically representing the healing power of Jesus Christ that can be easily put in place by sacristans. The oil of the sick may be moved from the ambry to another place of prominence such as a special stand near the presidential chair.

Christian Funerals

As with weddings, those who meet with families to plan a funeral should know the parish policies so that they can explain them well and encourage the family to celebrate fully the beautiful funeral rites of the Church. Booklets or other documents that communicate information about funeral planning, including elements such as music, wake services, and lunches, along with environment expectations, should be given to the family during the planning meeting. They could also be made available to parishioners at less emotional times as a way of helping them think about the future.

Does your church have space for wake services? Many families want to display photos or slide shows of the deceased; make sure you have easels, tables, or other spaces where these can be displayed in the narthex. Some funerals will produce myriad floral arrangements. Make sure there is a plan for placing these within the existing environment. Others may request donations in lieu of flowers, so have a plan for using plants and other elements in your environment to honor the deceased.

At funerals, the paschal candle is lit; the casket is covered with a white pall and sprinkled with holy water to remind the faithful of baptism. Often the casket is incensed during the final commendation. If the deceased has been cremated, the urn can be carried into the church in procession, just as the casket is, and placed on a stand or table in approximately the same position that the casket would occupy. (There is no analogous version of the pall for an urn.) Design a liturgical environment that makes these elements visible and accessible to participants.

Liturgy of the Hours

Praying the Liturgy of the Hours does not require special attention to the environment, but if your parish wishes to draw attention to this important prayer of the Church for a particular season or time, you may be asked to enhance the environment in some way. Keep in mind the antiphonal nature of the prayer when choosing the space you will use. A small table covered with a seasonally appropriate color of cloth, candles, and an open incense pot adds formality to this universal ritual.

Devotions

Devotions properly flow from and lead to a fuller participation in liturgy. Liturgical environment team members may be called on to help draw emphasis to particular devotions. Care must always be taken to keep the emphasis on devotional elements proportionately smaller than the emphasis on liturgy.

Decorating a separate chapel as you routinely decorate the church assures that the chapel is dressed for the Rite of Eucharistic Exposition and Benediction. Special times of adoration within a church would call for no adaptation of the environment. The Blessed Sacrament, exposed in the monstrance, should be the central focus. Adding floral arrangements or other items that are not usually in place will draw attention to themselves—and away from Christ whom we adore in the Blessed Sacrament.

Marian Devotions

Marian devotions, particularly a May crowning, may require moving the statue of Mary to a location that gives better access. Mary's role as the Mother of God has always been to draw the faithful close to her Son. In choosing a place of honor for Mary, take care not to place the statue of Mary in the line of vision between those gathered and the tabernacle or the altar.

This simple devotional space related to the Good Shepherd caring for the sheep does not distract from the liturgy.

Following the crowning, return the statue to its usual location. Add flowers, fabric, or ribbons, particularly during those months especially devoted to Mary: May and October.

A devotional chapel provides a good space for praying the Rosary; if the chapel is too small, consider designating a section of pews near a statue of Mary for this prayer. In placing statues within the church, take care to situate them appropriately for liturgy. Taking the prayer to the space reserved for Mary (or other saints) rather than moving the statue to the space used for liturgy gives continuity to the devotional prayer and forms the faithful further in the centrality of liturgy.

Many cultures have specific Marian devotions. Inquire about them and learn whether you could lend support through the liturgical environment.

Stations of the Cross

Traditionally prayed on Fridays during Lent, the Stations of the Cross may be accented with somber ribbons, rope, or fabric during Lent. Rather than individually decorating the stations, consider creating an illusion of the pilgrimage that the stations represent by running a length of ribbon or satin rope from one to the other. Let the effect be simple, in keeping with the unadorned tone of the Lenten season.

As the stations are prayed, it is customary for servers to carry a cross and candles through the church, stopping at each station. Make sure the cross and candles used for this purpose are lightweight so that the servers can manage them gracefully for the duration of the prayer.

Digital Media in the Liturgical Environment

Roman Catholic liturgy is celebrated according to universal guidelines carefully discerned and passed on over its long tradition. This may explain why, although digital media has been used in the worship services of many evangelical and some mainstream Protestant communities for some time, it has been less evident in Roman Catholic liturgy. Some Catholic churches do use it, however, and others may be considering its use. The spirit and specifics of the Church's liturgical law most relevant to this issue are expressed chiefly in documents already discussed: *Sacrosanctum concilium* (SC), the *General Instruction of the Roman Missal* (GIRM), and *Built of Living Stones: Art, Architecture, and Worship* (BLS). Since none of these discusses digital media specifically, however, Catholic communities considering its use will need to study and understand the principles expressed in those texts and discern how they apply to their particular circumstances.[24] A few dioceses have formulated policies that may help, but the general principles that underlie Catholic liturgy should set the tone for any discussion.[25]

What uses of digital media do communities generally consider?

- Projecting information onto a screen or wall—information such as the words or music of hymns, announcements, or cues for the assembly[26]

- Projecting a short video during or after a homily, such as an annual fundraising video for the parish or from the bishop, or for some other catechetical purpose

- Less often, decorating the interior walls of the church with projected images

Thinking through the Issues—Things to Consider

Since the Church considers the Mass to be the "center of the whole Christian life for the Church both universal and local, as well as for each of the faithful individually" (GIRM, 16), the physical setting in which it is celebrated must be conducive to this vital activity. In *Built of Living Stones*, the document pertaining specifically to the liturgical environment, certain words occur

---

24. One of the few books relevant to this topic is Eileen Crowley's *Liturgical Art for a Media Culture* (Collegeville, MN: Liturgical Press, 2007). The author, who is associate professor of liturgy, arts, and communication at Catholic Theological Union in Chicago, focuses on the use of digital media as liturgical art. For a broader, more theoretical perspective on the implications of digital media for liturgy, see the work of Teresa Berger, professor of liturgical studies, Yale Divinity School, including @ *Worship, Liturgical Practices in Digital Worlds* (London and New York: Routledge, 2017).
25. Two examples are the worship offices of the Diocese of Orlando, https://www.orlandodiocese.org/wp-content/uploads/2010/08/Projection-Guidelines_08.2015.pdf, and the Archdiocese of Milwaukee, https://www.archmil.org/ArchMil/Resources/ParCnl1/Manuals-for-Parishes/VideoTechnologyGuidelines.
26. Whenever texts are projected, communities will need to seek permission from all copyright holders.

repeatedly throughout the text: mystery, awe, beauty, reverence, dignity, authenticity, and noble simplicity. These are the touchstones for judging appropriateness in the liturgical environment. To be more specific, "The quality of appropriateness is demonstrated by the work's ability to bear the weight of mystery, awe, reverence, and wonder that the liturgical action expresses and by the way it serves and does not interrupt the ritual actions that have their own structure, rhythm, and movement" (BLS, 148).

Such care for the environment is warranted since the liturgy is the occasion, after all, in which "Christ is really present in the very assembly gathered in his name, in the person of the minister, in his word, and indeed substantially and uninterruptedly under the Eucharistic species" (GIRM, 27). The symbolic actions, gestures, postures, and objects of the liturgy make Christ's presence manifest to the people. Elements under consideration for the liturgical environment must be in harmony with this vocabulary of signs and symbols.

Yet another important principle to consider when deliberating about digital media is that the full, conscious, and active participation of the faithful must be enriched and not hindered. And finally, just as Christ is really present in the liturgy and the people are truly present by virtue of their full participation, all the elements of the liturgy must be genuine also—such as candles with a "living flame" (BLS, 92–93) in preference to electric lights made to look like candles, and living rather than artificial flowers and plants (BLS, 129).

Although it may seem convenient or pastoral to provide the texts of the Mass on a large screen for all to see, there are several reasons this would not be so. First, liturgy is a live event, intended to provide an experience set apart from ordinary life, where screens have become so prominent.[27] Second, digital media has an impact on the liturgical environment and the liturgy—whether simply words, or images and videos projected on screens or walls.

Screens, projectors, cameras, and cords may seem to be part of the utilitarian infrastructure of the church, like lights or sound equipment, but anything that is visible to the assembly has an impact on the liturgical environment. In addition, any text, images, or videos that are projected (whether on screens or walls) also become part of the visual landscape.

Because of this, the community will want to consider all aspects of digital media in the light of criteria applied to other aspects of the liturgical environment.

---

27. This is the reasoning of the Bishops Committee on Divine Worship, which does not give permission for projecting words from liturgical books, such as *The Roman Missal* or *Lectionary for Mass*, during the Mass. They discern that in the liturgy, the people participate more effectively by listening together attentively to the proclamation of God's Word, rather than reading it from a screen. Those who have hearing problems should, of course, have the option of reading the text from a book.

- The most crucial question is: Does the digital media under consideration serve or distract from the liturgy? Does it support the mystery, awe, beauty, reverence, dignity, authenticity, and noble simplicity of the liturgy?
- If screens, projectors, or cameras are visible, do they block or detract from other elements in the liturgical environment?
- Does the use of digital media (such as the movement of the screen or the changing images on the screen) in any way distract from the liturgical action?
- Is it beautiful? (How does the appearance of the print on the large screen compare with a simply bound hymnal or missal furnished in the pews?)
- Does the intended use of digital media truly promote full, conscious, and active participation of the assembly, or is participation in any way hindered?

Communities might be considering a particular kind of still image or video to be used in a different way in the liturgy—as art, for meditation.[28] This would, of course, require very careful consideration, selection, and discussion. *Built of Living Stones* instructs that art used in the liturgy should "evoke wonder at its beauty" and "lead beyond itself to the invisible God" (148).

Some in the community may see digital media as a tool for evangelization, thinking it might attract seekers who are comfortable with digital media in their daily lives. Catholic liturgy, however, invites people to enter into a time and space that is deliberately different from the secular world—into a state of mind that is set apart from everyday life.

Communities might want to consider the use of digital media for worship occasions and spaces other than the Mass in the church. Some digital media that would not be appropriate for use during Mass might be effective for prayer services, retreats, or times of reflection. Perhaps spaces other than the church itself might accommodate the use of digital media. For example, your community might decide that the gathering space (which assembly members encounter before moving into the church) would be appropriate for digital media and art.

Other issues to consider:[29]

- What are the specific needs you wish to fulfill?
- How strong is the interest in media technology in your community?

---

28. Crowley makes her case for this type of media art in a 2006 paper presented at Valparaiso University and available in this online collection: https://scholar.valpo.edu/cgi/viewcontent.cgi?article=1114&context=ils_papers.

29. Some of the points included here come from Crowley's *Liturgical Art for a Media Culture*, already cited.

- What process of assessment (initial and ongoing) might the community use—perhaps entrusted to the liturgy committee and pastor?
- What level of technology (what specific equipment) would be appropriate for your needs and budget—keeping in mind that costs will go beyond the initial investment?
- Do you have staff or volunteers with training and motivation to maintain the equipment and use of the technology?
- Wherever and whenever digital media is used, can the space accommodate the technical requirements—sources of electricity, positioning of projector, screen, and so forth—and would the equipment needed disrupt the ambiance you hope to create?
- Keep in mind that if digital media intended as liturgical art is used continuously, it becomes ordinary and may lose the effect intended.
- In all considerations, keep the characteristics and requirements of the liturgy uppermost.

Whatever the various positions of your community members on these questions, it will be important to help everyone understand the nature of the liturgy as described in the documents and to listen carefully to each other as you discern whether or how to move forward with digital media.

Conclusion

A young woman was giving a tour of her church to her fiancé's mother. They were discussing the lengths of black rope suspended from the skylights that formed the Lenten decor that year. "These won't be here for the wedding," the young woman assured her future mother-in-law. "We're getting married in Ordinary Time, so the church will have green. With my neutral palette, it will look nice." The work of the liturgical environment team had formed her well; she and her friends had all been recruited at various times during their childhood to help prepare the church for a changing season. Now young adults, they periodically gathered for a meal at which the conversation often shifted to "remember when" topics. Just as they intuitively anticipate the singing of "O, Come, O Come Emmanuel" during the Advent season, and recall homilies from their first Communion celebrations, they predict the water image banners that hang at Easter and vigorously debate the meaning of new elements such as the Lenten ropes.

In the Gospel according to John, we hear that the world could not contain all the books it would take to tell of all Jesus' miracles (John 21:25). It is also true that no single parish could contain the rich heritage of God's love expressed in the myriad cultures he created. We can appreciate the presence of God in each of them, though. We can listen and learn from each other, work together as children of God, and create spaces and places in our parishes and our hearts for the innumerable ways humans, throughout time and space, seek to praise and worship our God.

The work you do as a member of the liturgical environment team, with the help of the Holy Spirit, will bear much fruit. By surrounding God's holy people with beautifully accented symbols of the liturgy, with colors, shapes, and scents that engage the senses and stimulate memories, you help them enter more fully into the mysteries of the faith.

Questions for Discussion and Reflection

1. How do you distinguish between your personal tastes and the needs of the liturgy? The needs of the community? In what specific instances have you been able to do that? What would help you do it better?

2. What are the first questions to ask when planning and preparing? How have they led you (or how might they lead you) to a fulfilling outcome?

3. What gaps in knowledge about the liturgy do you or your team need to fill in? What skills do you need to develop? How might you do that?

4. Which racial and ethnic groups are represented in your parish? How aware are you of their customs and practices? How could they be brought into the work of the liturgical environment team so that their needs were better supported?

5. In general, how does the team communicate with assembly members and solicit feedback?

6. What methods of long term planning and evaluation do your team use? How might you improve them?

7. When you visit other churches, what elements of the liturgical environment and the art help (or hinder) your prayer?

Chapter 4

Spirituality and Discipleship

*Effective liturgical signs have a teaching function and encourage full,
conscious, and active participation, express and strengthen faith,
and lead people to God. . . . They also touch and move a person to
conversion of heart and not simply to enlightenment of mind.*

—*Built of Living Stones, 26*

To serve your church well as a minister of the liturgical environment, you will want to tend your own spiritual life. You have already encountered God in your prayer, in things that are beautiful, and in people who are good. You have experienced anxiety and pain, joy and exuberance. You have known moments of distance from God, as well as times of deepest intimacy. As you work with the art and environment of a church, you interact with the seasons of the year, the story of Christ, and the lives of the saints. You bring your own emotional and religious experience into the public arena of common worship. There, your Christian brothers and sisters will have a deeper experience of the God who became like us.

Many people who are drawn to this ministry feel a special attraction to holy places. Perhaps this psalm will resonate for you.

> How lovely your dwelling,
> O LORD of hosts!
> My soul yearns and pines
> for the courts of the LORD.
> My heart and flesh cry out
> for the living God.
> As the sparrow finds a home
> and the swallow a nest to settle her young,
> My home is by your altars,
> LORD of hosts, my king and my God!
> Blessed are those who dwell in your house!
> They never cease to praise you.

Psalm 84:2–5

Spirituality of Sunday Mass: Scriptures and Symbols

The foundation of your spiritual life is the Sunday Eucharist, where you experience the incarnate Word of God. Jesus speaks in the Gospel, and he shares his Body and Blood at the sacrifice of the altar. You join with the community of the faithful. You receive the nourishment you need to bring Christ to all you meet throughout the coming week.

You build on Sunday's worship through daily prayer and service. Pray at the start and close of the day, before meals, or when going from one place to another. Thank God for the gift of life and for the talents you have received. Ask for the grace to share them with a generous heart.

For example, you can use the texts for Sunday Mass for some of your daily prayer. Before a new season of the Church year begins, study the Sunday Scriptures. During Advent, the first readings are prophecies about the coming of Christ, and the second readings proclaim that he will come again. Pray over these texts. What symbols come to mind?

During Lent, the first readings trace key moments in the history of salvation. The other readings frequently issue a call to repentance. The Gospel readings on the third, fourth, and fifth Sundays of Year A are particularly appropriate for those who will be baptized at Easter. Pray with these passages. What do they say to you?

During the Easter season, the first readings all come from the Acts of the Apostles, and they tell how the word about Jesus spread. The Gospel readings present key images for the Eucharist of the community: Christ as its shepherd, and the anticipation of the Holy Spirit. What do these passages say to you?

Try the same exercise with some of the prayers from the Mass. Pray over the words you will hear the priest say after the invitation, "Let us pray." What images come to mind?

Another way to center yourself is to pray over some of the symbols of the season. You may do this exercise with others, perhaps the members of the liturgical environment team. Before Easter begins, for example, set a large bowl of water in your midst. Let everyone hear the proclamation of some of Scripture's great water stories. Pray in silence or with some music in the background. Share your thoughts—what comes to mind as you reflect on the gift of water? You may choose other Scriptures and symbols for the other seasons: to prepare for Advent, the prophecies of Isaiah or an icon of the pregnant Mary and the words of her Magnificat; for Lent, ashes and the Ash Wednesday words from the prophet Joel. Think over these and other primary symbols: light, incense, the lectionary, oil, bread, wine, the cross—what do they say about your beliefs? How can the environment of the church let these primary symbols speak?

A Formation in Beauty

Develop your own specific gifts and sharpen your visual sensitivities by studying various environments and the world of art.

Be alert to beautiful and interesting spaces around you. Observe how friends and family decorate their homes. Note how designers of places of business set an appropriate tone for the intended function of a space. Ask what makes contemporary dress fashionable, and what makes cosmetics effective.

Enjoy the world of nature. See how the city cares for its parks. Visit a botanical garden to experience the wealth of flora in the world, and notice how beautifully it can be arranged. Marvel at the sweeping hills in the country or the crash of waves along the shore. Explore the interplay of natural colors, shapes, and balances. These observations will expand the context in which you think about religious art and environment.

Whenever possible, take the opportunity to see great Christian art and architecture in person. If a nearby church or museum has a collection, go see it. Many civic museums display great religious art.

For hundreds of years, the greatest artists of Western Europe used their skills for the sake of the Gospel. Their work expressed their faith while it also captured and advanced Western civilization.

However, every culture and time used its genius for this purpose—not just Western European civilization. The worlds of art and religion naturally support each other. When you encounter great works of art from any century and any place, you stand at the threshold of the creative genius that God shares with humans. To meet great art is to brush against the Creator of all.

Visit a cathedral, church, museum, or any collection of Christian art. The very act of going there makes this a religious pilgrimage. Whether you cross the street or fly to a global urban center, moving your entire body from one place to another shows a sense of purpose and direction, a small step in the long journey toward the new Jerusalem.

When you arrive at a chapel or gallery of art, take your time before each image. What story does it tell? What message is it conveying? How does it do that? Who are the religious figures? How are they identified? What makes it art? How did the artist use materials? What makes the result a thing of beauty? How might it change the viewer into a believer?

Before you leave any work of religious art, let it nurture your faith. Engage it not as an art critic, but as a Christian. Let it speak to you. Let it guide you into God's presence.

You can find reproductions of great Christian art on the internet, in books, and on posters.[1] You can see television specials and play DVDs about great artists and their work. These valuable sources explore the history of the representation of religious beliefs and values. By all means, spend time with these

---

1. See, for example, the excellent reproductions in *An Illustrated History of the Church* by Guy Bedouelle (Chicago: Liturgy Training Publications, 2006). Any public library will have books about Christian art with color reproductions. For internet images, type "Christian art" into your search engine and click on "images."

materials too. They are no substitute, however, for seeing the real thing. You cannot walk around a picture of a sculpture. You cannot see the textures of paint and the subtle shades of color when you only look at a reproduced poster of an original portrait. Your faith can grow from seeing reproductions, but whenever possible, go see the originals.

Understanding Christian Art

You can enhance your appreciation of religious art by knowing your faith from the doctrines of the Church to the lives of the saints. You are already familiar with the basic tenets of the Creed, but you may not know some of the conventions artists use. A good dictionary of saints and symbols can guide you through this special visual language (see an example in the resource section). Through it you would learn, for example, that if you see an image of a bearded, bald man dressed in a robe, holding a book and a sword, you are seeing a representation of St. Paul. If a figure sporting a curly white beard and dressed in blue and gold is holding two keys, you know it is St. Peter. A young man in a pink robe is St. John. A woman with a spiked wheel is St. Catherine of Alexandria, who overcame the instrument of her torture. A woman holding a monstrance is St. Clare of Assisi. Such artwork is catechetical, and it should deepen your desire not just to learn about the saints, but to follow their example.

Prayer

Some beautiful prayers can be found in the *Book of Blessings*. These texts are used for the blessing of new works of art in churches, but they can also guide your prayer in the presence of these images.

This introduction comes from the Order for the Blessing of an Image of Our Lord Jesus Christ. Use it as you pray before an image of the Son of God.

> This image honors, above all, the truth that Christ is the visible image of the invisible God. The eternal Son of God, who came down to the womb of the Virgin Mary, is the sign and sacrament of God the Father. As Christ himself said: "He who sees me sees the Father." Therefore when we honor this image, let us lift up our eyes to Christ, who reigns for ever with the Father and the Holy Spirit.[2]

The following prayer comes later (1272) in the same order of service. Place yourself before an image of Christ in your parish church and offer this prayer for all who gaze on it for spiritual strength.

---

2. *Book of Blessings* (BB), 1265.

Lord,
listen to our prayer.
As your faithful people honor this image of your Son
        may they be of one mind with Christ.
May they exchange the image of the old Adam of earth
        by being transformed into Christ,
        the new Adam from heaven.
        May Christ be the way that leads them to you,
        the truth that shines in their hearts,
the life that animates their actions.
May Christ be a light to their footsteps,
a safe place of rest on their journey,
and the gate that opens to them the city of peace.

The prayers of the liturgy often use the images and symbols of Scripture precisely because of their great power to evoke God's presence in our midst. Reflect on this excerpt from the blessing for the water in the Order of Baptism of Children (54). Notice how it prepares you to sense God's presence in the baptismal water and to recollect the effect of your own baptism.

O God, who by invisible power
accomplish a wondrous effect
through sacramental signs
and who in many ways have prepared water, your creation,
to show forth the grace of Baptism;

O God, whose Spirit
in the first moments of the world's creation
hovered over the waters,
so that the very substance of water
would even then take to itself the power to sanctify . . .

O God, who caused the children of Abraham
to pass dry-shod through the Red Sea,
so that the chosen people,
set free from slavery to Pharaoh,
would prefigure the people of the baptized;

O God, whose Son . . .
as he hung upon the Cross,
gave forth water from his side along with blood . . .
Look now, we pray, upon the face of your Church
and graciously unseal for her the fountain of Baptism.

May this water receive by the Holy Spirit
the grace of your Only Begotten Son,
so that human nature, created in your image
and washed clean through the Sacrament of Baptism
from all the squalor of the life of old,
may be found worthy to rise to the life of newborn children
through water and the Holy Spirit.

May the power of the Holy Spirit,
O Lord, we pray,
come down through your Son
into the fullness of this font,
so that all who have been buried with Christ
by Baptism into death
may rise again to life with him.
Who lives and reigns for ever and ever.
Amen.

As you come to feel the power of the images and symbols of Scripture and liturgy at work in yourself, you will be increasingly sensitive to their role in the liturgical environment.

Scripture

The Bible, of course, is the ultimate source for our spiritual growth. Its images and symbols continually attract us, pulling us closer to the mysteries that no words can fully explain. As a minister engaged in the creative process, you might want to meditate on Psalm 104, a prayer to God the Creator.

Colossians 1:15 offers a thought-provoking perspective on this aspect of your work: Christ "is the image of the invisible God." Christ was perfectly what ministers of the environment can only strive to create: a visual image that leads humans to God.

The New Testament includes several passages that will inspire meditation on the ministry of the liturgical environment. Look these up in your Bible. Ask yourself how art and environment play a role in each passage. What does this text say to you? How does it affirm and challenge you as a disciple of Jesus?

While St. Paul was preaching in Lystra, he healed a man who had never walked in his life (Acts 14:13). The crowds wrongly assumed that Paul and his companion Barnabas were human representatives of the false gods they had been worshipping, Hermes and Zeus. The priests of Zeus brought oxen and garlands to honor them, and Paul and Barnabas impatiently explained that they were messengers, not gods.

This passage shows the instinct even among pagan worshippers to use garlands as an offering to God. When you decorate the church or an image with flowers, you follow the same instinct. You offer what is most beautiful from the earth to the one you most want to please. But you want your efforts to please God, not to draw undue attention to anyone else.

In Matthew 25:7, Jesus tells a parable of ten bridesmaids, five of whom were foolish, and five who were wise. When the bridegroom arrived unexpectedly, the foolish ones had insufficient oil, but the wise ones had planned ahead. At the all-important moment, the wise bridesmaids got up and trimmed their lamps.

The preparation of a space for worship requires advance planning. When people walk into a decorated space, they are taken aback by the beauty of it in a single instant. But that instant took many hours of preparation. When you prepare the church for worship, you are planning ahead, and when Christ the bridegroom comes in the sacraments, your trimmed lamps are burning bright to greet him.

In Matthew 12:44 and Luke 11:25, Jesus uses the image of a clean house to speak about a unique and unfair challenge in the spiritual life. He says that an unclean spirit can be driven away from a person, but it remains restless and looks for a place to continue its evil. When it rediscovers the person it left, it finds a tidily swept domain. It recruits seven other evil spirits, and they all take up residence there.

Whenever we overcome sin, we must be careful not to return to it. Sometimes we go back to our sin more strongly than before. We are tempted to think we have overcome evil when we may not have completely done so. When you prepare the church, when you make it clean and tidy, you perform a great spiritual service. But you will still confront the force of seven demons luring you to the sins of pride, self-pity, and materialism. Keep focused on Christ.

In 1 Timothy 2:9 and 1 Peter 3:3, the apostles make a series of recommendations to various subgroups of Christians. The parts addressed to women sound sexist by today's standards, but the advice is good if today's men also heed it. The letters say women should dress modestly without jewelry or expensive clothes. Good works and a gentle spirit are the proper "garments" that show respect for God.

When we prepare churches for liturgy, we may want to use the most expensive material available. But is lavish decoration the goal? The people are best drawn into the liturgy and God is best praised with authenticity—when the environment has helped convey to the people some aspect of the mysteries of the liturgy. That happens when the ministers are focused on authentic meanings rather than surface decorations.

Near the end of the Bible (Revelation 21:2, 19), John sees a vision of a new Jerusalem, prepared as a bride adorned for her husband. The foundations of its wall are decorated with every kind of jewel, making it more beautiful even than the temple used to be.

We all await our entry into the eternal dwelling place God has prepared for us. This Scripture describes the new Jerusalem as a city of incomparable beauty. Its extravagant decoration tells us it is the source of all that is beautiful and good. Whenever we stretch beyond surfaces to the source, no matter how much or little we budget for it, beauty will inspire worshippers to draw closer to God and to live by the Gospel. Then our church building will signify the new Jerusalem, and we the Church will signify the buildings where we worship. Our very selves will glow with the radiance of all that is good and beautiful about God.

Questions for Reflection and Discussion

1. What approach to your ministry would help you to center yourself spiritually and gain insight into the season or day for which you are preparing?

2. Recall a particular liturgical environment that you thought was effective. What made it so? How did it evoke a season, a feeling, an insight?

3. What traditions have you established for the decoration of your home? When do you take time to make it special? What ambiance are you trying to create? What effects work the best? Why?

4. When has your church building seemed especially conducive to the liturgy? What do you think made it so? How does the building and the environment you prepare in it help assembly members sense the presence of Christ in the liturgy? What could you do to help them more fully feel that presence?

5. In what ways does your ministry of liturgical environment help you and the assembly members better fulfill your mission as disciples of Christ? How does the liturgical environment help send you forth on mission?

Frequently Asked Questions

1. Everyone seems to have a different idea about how the church should be decorated. It's disheartening to hear complaints, to have to answer questions, and to listen to all the suggestions from parishioners. What should I say when people corner me to talk about these matters?

Talking with parishioners about the liturgical environment is an important part of the work of the liturgical environment team. Listening sympathetically and carefully to the complaints and suggestions will help you understand how people are interpreting the environments you prepare. It will tell you whether your intentions are getting through and perhaps suggest areas where liturgical catechesis might be approached through bulletin inserts or adult formation sessions. Your patience and interest will also convey to parishioners that you truly care what they think and eventually it will help them to be more receptive to your ideas.

2. The to-do list for the liturgical environment during Lent and Easter seems overwhelming and our team is small. How can we possibly get everything done?

You can't do it all yourselves! The team has to do the planning well in advance and then become recruiters and organizers—pulling in as many members of the community as possible to help with the tasks. Not only will this lighten your load, it will build community and heighten every participant's understanding and pleasure in the liturgy.

3. There is so much to learn about the liturgy and our team is made up of untrained volunteers. What's the most efficient way to learn what we need to know?

Consult your diocesan office of worship for advice about someone you could consult on a regular basis and for information about workshops, days of reflection, or conferences you could attend. Try to connect with or build a network of ministers of liturgical environment in nearby parishes. As you learn, also draw confidence from the formation that you have absorbed from your experiences as a practicing, involved member of the parish community.

4. Sometimes our team has a plan in the works that gets changed at the last minute by someone on the staff or in one of the other ministries. It's very frustrating! What can we do to prevent this?

It's very important to coordinate your plans with the other liturgical ministers and staff. Be sure a representative of your team attends the meetings of the parish liturgy committee or consults regularly with someone from the staff and the other liturgical ministries. Over time you will come to know the concerns of the other participants in liturgy preparation, but it's always smart and considerate to communicate frequently with everyone concerned. Charity is paramount in any ministry and keeps us focused on our ultimate goals.

Resources

Key Liturgical Documents for Liturgical Environment

Sacrosanctum concilium. The first document of the Second Vatican Council, promulgated on December 4, 1963, also known by its English title, *Constitution on the Sacred Liturgy*. It allowed the celebration of liturgical rites to the vernacular, called for the full, conscious, and active participation of the assembly, and ordered the revision of all liturgical rites.

General Instruction of the Roman Missal. The introductory document, or praenotanda, that explains the theological background and gives the directions for celebrating the Mass. It appears at the beginning of *The Roman Missal* and is also published separately.

Built of Living Stones: Art, *Architecture, and Worship*; Guidelines of the United States Conference of Catholic Bishops. Promulgated in 2000, it replaced a previous document called Environment and Art in Catholic Worship. It primarily provides detailed guidance for parishes engaged in the building or renovation of a church, explaining the theology of church architecture, art, and furnishings, and emphasizing that their overarching purpose is to serve the sacred rites that take place within it. This document is also essential reading for ministers of liturgical environment who prepare the church for worship throughout the liturgical year.

Directory on Popular Piety and the Liturgy: Principles and Guidelines. Published in 2001 by the Congregation for Divine Worship and the Discipline of the Sacraments, this document affirms the efficacy of devotional practices, and provides guidelines to ensure that they are in harmony with the liturgy but distinct from it.

Anthologies of Documents and USCCB Resources

The Liturgy Documents, Volume One, Fifth Edition: Essential Documents for Parish Worship. Chicago: Liturgy Training Publications, 2012.

An anthology of church documents, including (among others) such essentials as *Sacrosanctum concilium* (1963), *General Instruction of the Roman Missal* (2002), *Lectionary for Mass: Introduction* (1981, 1998), *Universal Norms on the Liturgical Year and the General Roman Calendar* (2002, 2010, 2011), *Sing to the Lord: Music in Divine Worship* (2007), and *Built of Living Stones* (2000).

The Liturgy Documents, Volume Two, Second Edition: Essential Documents for Parish Sacramental Rites and Other Liturgies. Chicago: Liturgy Training Publications, 2012.

> Find here the praenotanda (introductions) to rites of Christian initiation, confirmation, penance, pastoral care of the sick, the Order of Christian Funerals, and more—all of which can be helpful when preparing liturgical environments for these rites.

The Liturgy Documents, Volume Four: Supplemental Documents for Parish Worship, Devotions, Formation and Catechesis. Chicago: Liturgy Training Publications, 2013.

> A few items in this diverse collection may be of interest to ministers of liturgical environment, namely Pope John Paul II's Letter to Artists, Pope Benedict XVI's apostolic exhortations on the Eucharist and the Word of God, and several documents on popular piety and inculturation.

Popular Devotional Practices: Questions and Answers. United States Conference of Catholic Bishops, 2003.

> A convenient, concise overview, found on the USCCB website. Search for it by title with your search engine.

"Prayer and Worship"—Resources on the Website of the United States Conference of Catholic Bishops, usccb.org.

> On the website of the USCCB, allow your cursor to hover over the tab "Prayer and Worship," then choose from a list of categories to see many helpful resources.

Ritual Books

National Conference of Catholic Bishops. *Lectionary for Mass for Use in the Dioceses of the United States of America.* 2nd typical ed.

> Vol. 1, Sundays, Solemnities, Feasts of the Lord and the Saints.
>> Year A. Chicago: Liturgy Training Publications, 1998.
>> Year B. Chicago: Liturgy Training Publications, 1998.
>> Year C. Chicago: Liturgy Training Publications, 1998.
>
> Vol. 2, Weekdays, Year 1, Proper of Saints, Common of Saints. Chicago: Liturgy Training Publications, 2001.
>
> Vol. 3, Weekdays, Year 2, Proper of Saints, Common of Saints. Chicago: Liturgy Training Publications, 2001.
>
> Vol. 4, Common of Saints, Ritual Masses, Masses for Various Needs, Votive Masses, Masses for the Dead. Chicago: Liturgy Training Publications, 2001.

National Conference of Catholic Bishops. *Book of the Gospels for Use in the Dioceses of the United States of America.* 2nd typical ed. Chicago: Liturgy Training Publications, 2001.

> The *Lectionary* is the ritual book from which lectors and readers proclaim the readings at Mass. The Book of the Gospels is sometimes carried by a lector or reader if a deacon is not present.

Lectionaries—Study Editions

Lectionary for Mass, Sundays, Solemnities, Feasts of the Lord and Saints, Study Edition. Chicago: Liturgy Training Publications, 1970, 1998.

A paperback study edition of the first volume of the ritual edition of the Lectionary for Mass, this book will be a helpful reference for ministers of liturgical environment planning the seasons and needing access to the Sunday readings. Its appendixes contain tables of readings and responsorial psalms as well as dates of all Sundays and feasts for coming years.

The Weekday Lectionary: Study Edition. Chicago: Liturgy Training Publications, 2002.

This convenient and comprehensive paperback volume contains all of the readings for Weekday Masses, which are from the *Revised New American Bible* approved for use in the United States.

Scripture and Prayer

The Catholic Study Bible, Third Edition. Edited by Donald Senior, John J. Collins, and Mary Ann Getty. New York: Oxford University Press, 2010.

Since so many visual images important in the liturgy are based on Scripture, ministers of liturgical environment may benefit from this authoritative study Bible. It provides introductory essays on the historical, literary, and theological dimensions of Scripture and abundant footnotes that give historical explanations and clarify meaning. This Bible also includes an extensive reading guide for each book of the Bible, a concordance, indexes, and full-color maps.

At Home with the Word, Sunday Scriptures and Scripture Insights. Chicago: Liturgy Training Publications, published annually.

This annual publication contains the full text of all the readings for the Sundays of a given year (including the responsorial psalm), along with insights about the readings from Scripture scholars, questions for reflection and discussion, and suggestions for action steps.

Daily Prayer. Chicago: Liturgy Training Publications, published annually.

Using a familiar order of prayer (psalmody, Scripture, brief reflection, Prayer of the Faithful, Lord's Prayer, and closing prayer), this annual publication is ideal for personal and communal reflection on the Word of God.

Workbook for Lectors, Gospel Readers, and Proclaimers of the Word. Chicago: Liturgy Training Publications, published annually.

This is the tool many readers use to prepare to proclaim the Scripture on Sundays. The commentaries written by Scripture scholars are longer than the Scripture insights found in *At Home with the Word* and may serve the needs of ministers of liturgical environment who want to go deeper into the readings.

About the Liturgy

Driscoll, Jeremy. *What Happens at Mass, Revised Edition*. Chicago: Liturgy Training Publications, 2005.

> Abbot Jeremy Driscoll, OSB, leads the reader through the Mass, imparting a deeper understanding of the work of our salvation.

Huck, Gabe. *Liturgy with Style and Grace, Third Edition, Revised*. Chicago: Liturgy Training Publications, 2018

> This book contains very brief, eloquent pieces on many aspects of the liturgy, liturgical ministries, and the liturgical year by a classic author in pastoral liturgy.

Irwin, Kevin W. *Responses to 101 Questions on the Mass*. New York/Mahwah, New Jersey: Paulist Press, 1999.

> A scholar of sacramental theology answers questions about the Mass, giving authoritative but pastoral explanations.

Laughlin, Corinna. *The Liturgy: The Source and Summit of Our Christian Life*. Chicago: Liturgy Training Publications, 2018.

> The best place to begin learning about the liturgy, this brief, friendly book by one of the authors of this resource will give you a firm grasp of the most important characteristics of the Mass.

Pastoral Liturgy®. Liturgy Training Publications.

> This bimonthly, vividly illustrated magazine provides articles that deepen appreciation and understanding of parish liturgy for everyone involved in it.

Ruzicki, Michael, Victoria M. Tufano, D. Todd Williamson, and Terry Navarro. *Signs and Symbols of the Liturgy: An Experience of Ritual and Catechesis*. Chicago: Liturgy Training Publications, 2018.

> This book contains scripts, floorplans, detailed instructions, and access to videos showing how to present a poetic, contemplative, and mystagogical experience of the signs and symbols of the liturgy for groups large and small. Whether helping to present it, or experiencing it, liturgical environment ministers especially would appreciate this retreat-like exercise.

The Liturgical Year

The Catholic Planning Calendar. Chicago: Liturgy Training Publications, published annually.

> An oversized calendar that may be used on a wall or desk. It displays all pertinent liturgical information for the year, making it a perfect planning tool for all liturgical ministries.

Coffey, Cathy, et al. *Companion to the Calendar, Second Edition: A Guide to the Saints, Seasons, and Holidays of the Year*. Chicago: Liturgy Training Publications, 2012.

> A lively introduction to the liturgical year—its seasons, solemnities, feasts, memorials, and secular holidays as well. Short entries, some line drawings.

Liturgy and Appointment Calendar. Chicago: Liturgy Training Publications, published annually.

> A personal appointment calendar that displays liturgical information for each day, secular holidays, and days important to other religions.

The Year of Grace. Chicago: Liturgy Training Publications, published annually.

> A colorful, decorative poster-sized liturgical calendar in the shape of a wheel displays each day of the year and indicates seasons, solemnities, feasts and memorials. A different artist illustrates the calendar each year with a liturgical or scriptural topic. Explanations of the illustrated topic and the liturgical year are on the back of the calendar, also downloadable. This resource instructs as it enhances walls in the church narthex, parish center, school, or home.

Preparation of Liturgy and the Liturgical Environment

Mazar, Peter. *School Year, Church Year: Customs and Decorations for the Classroom.* Chicago: Liturgy Training Publications, 2001.

> Although focused on classrooms, this book will help parish ministers of liturgical environment advise and collaborate with parish school teachers and students who will inevitably interface with them on various occasions.

Sourcebook for Sundays, Seasons, and Weekdays: The Almanac for Pastoral Liturgy. Chicago: Liturgy Training Publications, published annually.

> This resource will take you day by day through the liturgical year, explaining the meanings of and many aspects of preparation necessary for each liturgy.

Mazar, Peter, with revisions by Rev. J. Philip Horrigan. *To Crown the Year: Decorating the Church through the Seasons, Second Edition.* Chicago: Liturgy Training Publications, 1995, 2015.

> A classic parish resource for preparing the liturgical environment—warm, inviting, humorous—full of wisdom and practical advice. Updated in 2015.

Ryan, G. Thomas, with revisions by Corinna Laughlin. *The Sacristy Manual, Second Edition.* Chicago: Liturgy Training Publications, 1992, 2011.

> Although ministers of liturgical environment are not usually sacristans, they will need to collaborate closely with the keeper of the sacristy, since they will be using and helping to care for many of the same things. This book contains a careful description of all the spaces and objects needed for the liturgy, with advice on choosing, storing, and caring for them. Checklists specify which items are needed for each liturgy, rite, or occasion.

History and Appreciation of Liturgical Art and Architecture

Bedouelle, Guy. *An Illustrated History of the Church*. Chicago: Liturgy Training Publications, 2006.

Although not a history of liturgical art and architecture, this book contains good quality reproductions of some church architecture and furnishings.

Foley, Edward. *From Age to Age: How Christians Have Celebrated the Eucharist, Revised and Expanded Edition*. Collegeville, MN: Liturgical Press, 2008.

A pastoral and comprehensive history of the Mass—its buildings, art, music, texts, and practices. This book is full of maps, photos of art and artifacts, drawings, floor plans, and reproductions of ancient music notation and primary documents, Despite the book's many details, the writing is inviting and interesting.

A History of the Mass / Una historia de la Misa. Chicago: Liturgy Training Publications, 2007.

This bilingual DVD traces the evolution of the Mass, showing how it was shaped and reshaped by the times, cultures, theology, and arts of each era.

Murray, Peter and Linda Murray. *The Oxford Companion to Christian Art and Architecture*. New York: Oxford University Press, 1998.

In this 624-page illustrated reference book, names of biblical persons, saints, symbols, artists, places, monuments, and topics related to the Christian arts are arranged alphabetically. Ministers of the liturgical environment, as well as others in parish ministry, would find this a very helpful resource to have in the church library. (Earlier editions may be purchased used from a variety of online booksellers.)

Pecklers, Keith F., SJ. *Liturgy: The Illustrated History*. Mahwah, NJ: Paulist Press; and Milan: Edioriale Jaca Book SpA, 2012.

A history of the liturgy, copiously illustrated with high quality reproductions of art from each period. Another mind-expanding reference book for ministers of liturgical environment and anyone involved in liturgical catechesis.

Taylor, Richard. *How to Read a Church: A Guide to Symbols and Images in Churches and Cathedrals*. Mahwah, NJ: Hidden Spring (Paulist), 2005.

In this modest paperback, many diagrams, line drawings, and a few photos supplement the categories of entries that describe parts and furnishings of church buildings, types of crosses, God, Jesus, Mary, saints, Scripture themes, animals, birds, letters, words, and vesture.

Liturgy in Multicultural Parishes

Francis, Mark R., CSV, with contributions by Rufino Zaragoza, OFM. *Liturgy in a Culturally Diverse Community: A Guide Toward Understanding.* Washington, DC: Federation of Diocesan Liturgical Commissions, 2012.

> This brief, bilingual guide (English and Spanish) begins with a rationale and principles for developing multicultural liturgies, then provides specific practical suggestions for each aspect of a multicultural celebration, including art and environment on pages 20–23.

Matovina, Timothy and Gary Riebe-Estrella, SVD, eds. *Horizons of the Sacred: Mexican Traditions in U.S. Catholicism.* Ithaca and London: Cornell University Press, 2002.

> This is a collection of essays that explores the lived experience and world view of Catholics with Mexican heritage living and practicing their faith in the United States.

Matovina, Timothy. *Latino Catholicism: Transformation in America's Largest Church.* Princeton and Oxford: Princeton University Press, 2012.

> This detailed history of Mexican Catholics living in the United States shows how both the people and the Church are evolving as they influence each other. It is likely too long and detailed for most, but still we benefit from knowing it exists.

United States Conference of Catholic Bishops Website, Resources on Multicultural Liturgies.

> The bishops offer a number of resources. To access them, type "USCCB" and "multicultural liturgy" into your search engine and explore from where you land.

United States Conference of Catholic Bishops Website, Resources on Black Catholics, Native American Catholics, Asian and Pacific Islander Catholics, and Hispanic/Latino Catholics.

> The bishops offer various resources on these Catholic groups. To access them, type "USCCB" and the name of each group into your search engine and explore from where you land.

Glossary

Advent: The liturgical time of joyful preparation and anticipation for Christmas. It is also a time of penance, although this aspect is secondary to the spirit of hope-filled waiting. This time, considered to be the start of a new liturgical year, begins on the fourth Sunday before Christmas.

Alb: A full-length white liturgical robe, from the Latin *albus*, meaning "white." The alb is the preferred vestment for all ministers, from server to bishop. It recalls the white garment put on at baptism as a sign of putting on the new life of Christ. Ordained ministers wear a stole and an outer garment over the alb.

Altar: The sacred table on which the sacrifice of the Mass is celebrated. It is the central symbol of Christ in a church building. In the United States, the table of the altar may be made of stone or wood; the base or supports may be made of any dignified and solid material. In new churches there is to be only one altar.

Ambo: The place from which all the Scripture readings are proclaimed and the homily may be preached during liturgy; a pulpit or lectern. The ambo is also used for the singing of the Exsultet, for announcing the intentions of the Universal Prayer, and for the leading of the responsorial psalm. The term is derived from a Greek word for "raised place."

Apse: A semicircular or rectangular space that is sometimes vaulted by a half dome. Often an apse is a part of or adjacent to the sanctuary. Sometimes statues or other devotional items are placed in an apse.

Ambry: A place for the storing of the holy oils (chrism, oil of catechumens, and oil of the sick). In older churches the ambry was a niche in the wall, often with a locking door. In new and renovated churches, the ambry is often located near the baptismal font and constructed so that the vessels containing the holy oils can be seen. It is also spelled aumbry.

Architecture, Liturgical: The form of architecture by which building designs meet the demands of the liturgical celebrations of the Church. New liturgical constructions must be designed in harmony with Church laws and must facilitate the full, conscious, and active participation of all in the liturgical action according to the various roles that make up the Body of Christ at worship. General principles along with specific requirements are described in chapter 5 of the *General Instruction of the Roman Missal* and, for the United States, in *Built of Living Stones: Art, Architecture, and Worship.*

Art, Liturgical: Any art form that serves the liturgy. Art that is appropriate for worship should be of good quality, express the divine presence, be appropriate for liturgical action, be able to bear the weight of mystery, and be made of genuine materials. Discussed in chapter 5 of the *General Instruction of the Roman*

Missal and, for the United States, in *Built of Living Stones: Art, Architecture, and Worship.*

Asperges: The rite of sprinkling holy water on the assembly at Mass. In the current Roman Missal, where it is called the Rite for the Blessing and Sprinkling of Water, it may take the place of the penitential act, especially on the Sundays of Easter Time, as a reminder of baptism. The sprinkling of the assembly may be accompanied by Psalm 51, with the Latin antiphon that begins "Asperges me" ("Sprinkle me"), or by other antiphons or hymns. In the Tridentine rite, this sprinkling may take place before the formal start of a high Mass.

Assembly: The people gathered for divine worship, often called the congregation. The *Constitution on the Sacred Liturgy* (no. 7), discussing the many ways Christ is present in the sacrifice of the Mass, says, "He is present . . . when the Church prays and sings, for he promised: 'Where two or three are gathered together in my name, there am I in the midst of them' (Matthew 18:20)." Contemporary liturgical theology emphasizes that it is the assembly as a whole that celebrates the liturgy under the leadership of a priest.

Book of the Gospels: A ritual book from which the passages from the Gospels prescribed for Masses on Sundays, solemnities, feasts of the Lord and of the saints, and ritual Masses are proclaimed; also called an evangeliary. It may be carried in the entrance procession and placed on the altar, and then processed to the ambo during the Gospel Acclamation. It is presented to deacons at their ordination and held over the heads of bishops at their ordination.

Candle: A lamp that has a living flame. For the celebration of Mass, two, four, or six candles may be used, and seven may be used when the diocesan bishop celebrates Mass. Candles used for Mass must be made of wax.

Chalice: The sacred vessel, usually a stemmed cup, used to hold the wine that is consecrated during the Mass.

Chancel: Another name for the sanctuary, although in some churches the chancel may include the choir area in addition to the sanctuary.

Chasuble: The outer vestment of priests and bishops worn while celebrating the Eucharist. It is a large, sleeveless garment with a simple opening for the head worn over the stole and alb. The color of the chasuble matches the liturgical color of the feast or liturgical time.

Chrism: One of the three holy oils. It is consecrated by the bishop at the Chrism Mass and used at the baptism of infants, at confirmation, at the ordination of priests and bishops, and at the dedication of churches and altars. Chrism is scented, usually with balsam, which creates a distinctive and pleasing aroma; it is the only one of the three sacramental oils that is scented. Chrism is stored in the ambry and in oil stocks that are often labeled SC, for "sacred chrism."

Christmas Time: The period of the liturgical year beginning with Evening Prayer I of the Nativity of the Lord and ending with Evening Prayer on the Feast of the Baptism of the Lord (which may fall on the Sunday or Monday after

Epiphany). This liturgical time commemorates the incarnation, the birth of Christ, and his first manifestations.

Ciborium: The liturgical vessel used for the Eucharistic bread. Although many ciboria resemble chalices, contemporary ciboria are more commonly made in the form of bowls. Both styles frequently are made with a covering lid. The canopy or baldacchino over an altar is sometimes called a ciborium.

Corporal: A white linen cloth placed on top of the altar cloth during Mass. The chalice and paten are placed on top of the corporal.

Credence Table: The side table on which the vessels and articles needed for the celebration are placed when not in use, particularly during the celebration of the Eucharist.

Dalmatic: The sleeved outer vestment proper to a deacon, worn over the alb and stole. The color of the dalmatic matches the liturgical color of the feast or liturgical time.

Easter Time: The period of fifty days from the Easter Vigil until the conclusion of Evening Prayer on Pentecost. This liturgical time is celebrated with great joy and exultation as one great feast day, one great Sunday characterized especially by the singing of Alleluia.

Feast: A rank within the category of liturgical days, lower than a solemnity but higher than a memorial. Feasts usually do not include Evening Prayer I, but usually do have a complete proper set of texts for the Mass along with readings.

Funeral Mass: The principal liturgical celebration of the Christian community for the deceased. The liturgy begins with the greeting at the church entrance of the mourners who accompany the deceased, a sprinkling of the coffin with holy water, and the placing of the funeral pall on the coffin. After the entrance procession, a Christian symbol may be placed on the coffin. After the collect, the Liturgy of the Word and the Liturgy of the Eucharist are celebrated in the usual manner, and the Mass concludes with the Final Commendation. In the case of a funeral liturgy outside Mass, the Liturgy of the Word is celebrated and the Final Commendation follows the Universal Prayer and the Our Father.

Gaudete Sunday: Name given to the Third Sunday of Advent, taken from the first word of the entrance antiphon in Latin, *Gaudete*, "rejoice." Rose-colored vestments may be worn on this day instead of violet.

General Instruction of the Roman Missal **(GIRM):** The introductory document, or praenotanda, that explains the theological background and gives the directions for celebrating the Mass. It appears at the beginning of *The Roman Missal*, and it is also published separately.

Laetare Sunday: Name given to the Fourth Sunday of Lent, taken from the first word of the entrance antiphon in Latin, "Rejoice, Jerusalem." Rose-colored vestments may be worn on this day instead of violet, and flowers may be used to decorate the sanctuary.

Lectionary for Mass: The book containing the Scripture readings proclaimed at Mass, including the responsorial psalms, for each day of the year. The lectionary approved for use in the United States is published in several volumes. The Gospel readings are also contained in a separate Book of the Gospels.

Lent: The period that precedes the celebration of Christ's passion and resurrection during the Paschal Triduum. Lent is both a time of preparation for baptism and a penitential time; it is approximately forty days long, echoing the forty days of prayer and fasting of Jesus in the desert after his baptism. In the Western Church, it begins on Ash Wednesday and continues for six weeks. In the Byzantine Rite, it begins two days earlier, on the Monday prior to the First Sunday of Lent. It ends prior to the Evening Mass of the Lord's Supper on Holy Thursday. The last week of Lent is called Holy Week. For the elect, Lent is the Period of Purification and Enlightenment, the final preparation for baptism at Easter. For the baptized, Lent is a time for renewal in the meaning and grace of their own baptism. The Alleluia is not sung or said from the beginning of Lent until the Easter Vigil.

Liturgical color: Each season of the liturgical year and particular solemnities, feasts, and memorials are assigned colors. The color is generally reflected in the vestments of the priest and the decorations of the church.

Liturgical year: The marking of the calendar year with occasions that reveal the grace and mystery of the Trinity.

Liturgical Year: The annual cycle of liturgical celebrations, centered on the celebration of Easter. The liturgical year of the Roman Rite begins with the First Sunday of Advent. It comprises Advent, the four-week time of preparation for the Nativity of the Lord; Christmas Time, which extends from the Nativity of the Lord through the Baptism of the Lord; Lent, the six-week time of preparation for the Paschal Triduum; Easter Time, a fifty-day celebration of the resurrection which concludes with Pentecost; and Ordinary Time. Ordinary Time is divided into two segments; the first occurs between the end of Christmas Time and the beginning of Lent, and the second from Pentecost to the beginning of Advent. The feast days of the Lord and of the saints add additional variety and richness to the Church's liturgical year.

Memorial: (1) A common way of translating the word anamnesis and of understanding the concept. In liturgical theology, however, anamnesis is not understood as a memorial ceremony that merely recalls a past event. It is understood, rather, as the active remembrance and making present of a saving reality. (2) The rank of liturgical days lower than both solemnities and feasts. Memorials may be classified as either obligatory or optional. On the weekdays of Lent, the weekdays of Advent from December 17 to 24, and the days within the Octave of Christmas, all memorials are considered optional and may be observed only as commemorations.

Monstrance: The vessel used to display a large consecrated host during exposition of the Blessed Sacrament. While there are many different designs and styles for monstrances, it always has a base so that it can stand upright on a flat surface—e.g., the altar, and a clear round window where the lunette with the host is placed.

Narthex: The space inside the entrance of a church where people may gather before or after liturgy. It can be a place of welcome, a transitional space from the outside world into the worship space of the church, and vice versa. Some liturgical moments may occur in the narthex, such as the introductory rites of the Rite of Acceptance into the Order of Catechumens, of the Rite of Baptism for Children, and of the Funeral Liturgy.

Nave: The main section of a church building where the assembly gathers for worship. It is the area in the church building for the faithful containing the pews, distinct from the sanctuary.

Ordinary Time: The liturgical time that does not celebrate any particular aspect of the mystery of Christ, but rather the mystery of Christ in its fullness. It spans two periods of the liturgical calendar. The first period begins on the day following the Feast of the Baptism of the Lord and continues through the Tuesday before Ash Wednesday; the second begins on the day after Pentecost and continues until Evening Prayer I of the First Sunday of Advent. The term ordinary refers to the term ordinal, as in numerical, referring to the numerical titles given to the Sundays of this period, such as the Third Sunday in Ordinary Time.

Ordo: (1) A term used for the order or ordinary of the Mass, especially used of the Roman ordines, documents that described the early Roman liturgies. (2) A term that can be used interchangeably with rite to designate groups of rituals, as in the title Order of Christian Funerals. (3) The detailed annual liturgical calendar that indicates which liturgical celebrations occur on which days, and which texts can or must be used in the celebration of Mass and of the Liturgy of the Hours on a specific day.

Pall: (1) The large white cloth used to cover the coffin of the deceased during the funeral liturgy as a reminder of the baptismal garment. (2) A flat, cloth-covered board, about six inches square, used to cover the chalice to keep insects out. Its use is optional.

Paten: The name for the plate which holds the Eucharistic bread during Mass. Although the term is associated with a small, disk-like plate sized to hold only one large host for the priest, it can also be applied to a larger plate containing a sufficient amount of bread for the communion of the entire assembly. It is preferable to use only one large plate as a sign of the unity of the assembly and the offering of one sacrifice. A large paten would still be distinguished from a ciborium, however, in that a paten more resembles a plate, dish, or tray, whereas a ciborium resembles a cup or a bowl.

Pentecost: The fiftieth and final day of Easter Time; the eighth Sunday of Easter Time. Pentecost commemorates the descent of the Holy Spirit on the disciples as narrated in Acts 2:1–12. The celebration of Easter concludes with Evening Prayer on Pentecost and Ordinary Time resumes the next day.

Procession: Formal, ordered movement of people from one place to another.

Purificator: The cloth used to wipe the rim of the chalice containing the Blood of Christ after someone drinks from it during the celebration of the Eucharist. The purificator is usually rectangular in shape, folded lengthwise in thirds and then in half, and embroidered with a small red cross.

Roman Missal: The book or books containing the prayers, hymns, and Scripture readings prescribed for the celebration of Mass. Before the revision of the Missal in 1570, after the Council of Trent, the various texts were found in different books, but these were combined into one volume after the Council. The one-volume Missal was commonplace until the Second Vatican Council. The present-day Missal, published in 1970 and currently in its third edition, is subdivided into several books: a book of prayers used by the priest, which is still called the "Missal" even though technically the book contains only part of the Missal; the Lectionary, which contains the Scripture readings; and the book of hymns and antiphons called the Gradual.

Rubric: A direction or explanatory instruction printed between prayers or other spoken texts of a liturgical rite. The word rubric is derived from the Latin word for "red" because rubrics are normally printed in red in the liturgical books. Some rubrics are descriptive, and thus may be adapted in certain situations; and others are prescriptive, and thus must be carried out as written. Rubrics are meant to give structure and order to a ritual. The term is often used in the plural to speak of the norms or directives of a liturgy as a whole.

Sacramentals: Sacred signs, including words, actions, and objects that signify spiritual effects achieved through the intercession of the Church. Unlike the sacraments, which have been instituted by Christ, sacramentals are instituted by the Church. Sacramentals include blessings, medals, statues and other sacred images, palms, holy water, and many devotions, including the Rosary. They prepare us to receive the fruit of the sacraments and sanctify different circumstances of life (see *Catechism of the Catholic Church*, 1677).

Sacristan: The liturgical minister who has the responsibility for preparing everything needed for liturgical celebrations. The duties of the sacristan include arranging everything needed before the liturgy begins, and cleaning up and putting things away after. Sometimes his or her duties include caring for the sacristy, vestments, vessels, and the good order of the worship space itself. The ministry of sacristan is included in the Order for the Blessing of Altar Servers, Sacristans, Musicians, and Ushers in the Book of Blessings.

Sacristy: The room in which vestments and liturgical items are stored and prepared for use before liturgies. It is also commonly used as a vesting room, although larger churches and cathedrals may have a separate vesting room, called the secretarium.

Sanctoral cycle: Solemnities, feasts, and memorials of saints that are celebrated each year.

Sanctuary: The area of the church in which the presidential chair, altar, and ambo are located, and in which the primary ministers may also sit. Normally it is somewhat elevated, for the sake of visibility. It should be in some way distinct from the other areas of the church, yet at the same time integrally related to the entire space, to convey a sense of unity and wholeness. It is sometimes referred to as the presbyterium or chancel.

Solemnity: A category of liturgical day that is higher than a feast or a memorial. The celebration of a solemnity begins with Evening Prayer I on the preceding day. Some solemnities also have their own Vigil Mass, to be used on the evening of the preceding day if Mass is celebrated at that time. The two greatest solemnities are Easter and the Nativity of the Lord, each of which has an octave. On solemnities, the Glory to God in the Highest and the Profession of Faith are prescribed at Mass.

Stole: The vestment worn over the neck by ordained ministers. It is a long band of fabric about five inches wide. A priest or bishop wears the stole around the neck and hanging down in front. A deacon wears the stole over the left shoulder and fastened at his waist on the right side. At Mass, the stole is worn underneath the chasuble or dalmatic.

Surplice: A white, loose, tunic-like garment worn over a cassock. It is derived from the alb, and may be worn by priests when presiding at non-Eucharistic liturgies. In some parishes altar servers vest in cassock and surplice.

Tabernacle: The safe-like receptacle for storing the consecrated Eucharistic bread. When the Blessed Sacrament is present in the tabernacle, it is to be locked and the sanctuary light is to be lit. The tabernacle must be immovable, solid, and not transparent.

Te Deum: A hymn that begins with the words, "You are God, we praise you." It occurs at the end of the Office of Readings on Sundays (apart from Lent), during the octaves of Easter and Christmas, and on solemnities and feasts. It is also sung at the end of the Mass of the ordination of a bishop while the new bishop processes through the assembly to give his blessing and on other joyful occasions.

Temporal Cycle: A term sometimes used to refer to the portion of the liturgical calendar related to the liturgical times (Lent, Easter, Advent, Christmas, Ordinary Time). In contrast, celebrations associated with specific dates, apart from Christmas (such as the Annunciation on March 25), are sometimes called the sanctoral cycle.

Triduum: Literally, "three days"; another name for the Paschal Triduum.

Universal Prayer: The intercessory prayers in the celebration of the Mass, following the Creed on Sundays and solemnities or the homily on other days; also called the Prayer of the Faithful or Bidding Prayers, and formerly called the General Intercessions. It consists of an introduction, intentions and responses to the intentions, and a concluding prayer.

Vestments: The ritual garments and symbols of office worn by various ministers at liturgy. The vestment for all ministers in the sanctuary is the alb, over which ordained ministers add a stole. At the celebration of the Eucharist, bishops and priests wear a chasuble over the alb and stole, and a deacon wears a dalmatic. The cope, a long, cape-like vestment, is worn by ordained ministers over an alb and stole for solemn liturgies outside Mass. Copes may also be worn for solemn processions.

Vigil: A service held on the evening prior to the actual day. The greatest and most noble vigil is the Easter Vigil. Certain solemnities have their own Vigil Mass— i.e., Epiphany, Pentecost, the Nativity of St. John the Baptist, the Assumption of the Blessed Virgin Mary, and the Nativity of the Lord.

Prayer of Preparation for Ministers of Liturgical Environment

Good and gracious God,
your abundant love fills our world with things of beauty,
giving us glimpses of the splendor to come.
As we prepare to decorate for this season of _____ ,
      send your Holy Spirit to guide and grace us,
that the work we do may immerse your holy people
more fully into the mystery that is you.
Accept the gift of labor our hands will provide.
May our work, lovingly done,
bring us and the people we serve closer to you.
Grant this through Christ our Lord. Amen.